Autism Mom

New Ways of Thinking

Shirley Blaier-Stein

Shirley Blaier-Stein

AUTISM MOM

To protect other people's privacy and anonymity, I changed their names, circumstances and some other factual details. These changes do not compromise the truth of my story.

Cover design by Vanessa Maynard

Author photograph by Peter Friedman

ISBN: 978-0-615-91475-6

WWW DOT AUTISMMOMBOOK DOT COM

For Dan, with endless love

Contents

NEW WAYS OF THINKING

March 2010

One especially freezing Sunday morning in Connecticut, I found myself standing by the kitchen door, torn between my two children. Outside was Dan, my autistic six year old boy, and inside was Gali, my two year old baby girl.

Dan woke up at the crack of dawn and immediately started to cry loudly and hit his head with his hands. My husband Alex ran into his room. I didn't know what was going on in there until I heard Alex scream "No!" and saw him coming out of there with his hand on his face. Dan had punched him in the eye.

I tried to stay calm. All this meant was that Dan was having a hard time, and needed our help. He never meant to hurt any of us. I went in there to find Dan crying in deep sorrow. To me it felt as though he knew he had done something wrong, but could not control himself.

I tried to help him by pressing on his arms and legs, the way Dan's occupational therapist taught me. Deep pressure often helped him feel better. Three seconds into that, Dan punched me in my face too. Then he started spitting. My poor boy was out of control. Suddenly he stopped, stood up, and walked towards the hallway. I followed him downstairs, hoping he'd make his way into the kitchen. Eating usually helped. I would give him some breakfast, I thought. Alex followed us, carrying Gali in his arms. He got her settled in with her bottle and a DVD and joined us in the kitchen.

Dan was happy eating a Milano cookie. But when the three cookies that were left in the bag were gone, he returned to the same state he woke up in, completely disoriented.

"Awhaaaa haaaaaaaaaaa!" He screamed and flapped his arms around with no control, only ceasing from that to try and climb onto the kitchen counter.

Just then Alex's phone rang. It was my stepson Tomer calling to be picked up from his sleepover at a friend's house, a thirty minute drive away. 'What can I do?' said Alex's eyes as he left me alone in the kitchen with Dan. I felt like the air got sucked out of the room.

I offered Dan other food items, but he just kept on crying and running around the kitchen, ignoring me completely.

He finally stopped, stood by the kitchen door and started banging on the glass part. "Do you want to go outside?" I did not really think I would get an answer, but he got quiet for a short moment. It was enough for me to know he meant yes. I ran upstairs as fast as I could, to get Dan's clothes, almost tripping on the stairs, my heart racing. I got Dan dressed and he bolted out.

I decided to stay inside, by the door. I figured this way I could hear Gali and watch Dan at the same time. Our backyard was fenced, and if Dan tried to go to the street I would see him in time to catch him.

After a few seconds I heard him cry. He sounded so lonely in his pain. I had to be there for him. He wouldn't let me hug him or even touch him that morning, but I had to be there anyway.

Luckily, all that Gali wanted at this point was a pink lollipop and to continue watching the video. I kissed her blond curls and tucked away the guilt of feeding my baby pure sugar instead of real food. I decided to feed her a healthy breakfast later, when this raging storm that took over Dan had ended.

I ran outside with just my pajamas and slippers on. I did not feel the cold. I was in such emotional turmoil, so many feelings storming inside of me. I was desperate to help Dan; angry that this is happening to him; and sorry for myself. I felt powerless.

Dan was sitting on the swing, tears coming down his cheeks, screaming out loud. He usually liked it when I pushed his feet so I tried that. The brown cold mud from the bottom of Dan's blue boots stuck to my hands and got onto the front of my pajamas. I did not care. All I saw and all I heard at that moment was my boy in agony, and all I wanted was to help him. To find some magical way to relieve his suffering.

'Help,' I thought, 'please help me. Help me and help my boy.' I was not sure who I was "talking" to. I took a few steps towards my tree and placed my hands on its brownish-grayish-bumpy bark. This was a huge-old-strong oak that I always felt was guarding the property, watching over us. We would eat in its shade in the summer, run around it to play tag, hang Halloween decorations. Gali and I lay a blanket under it on Mother's day and had a picnic. I stood there for a brief moment, absorbing the tree's healing energy into me, and then I returned back to Dan at the swing.

Through Dan's wailing, my crying and the pain I felt, I could picture my friend Marina coming to stand by my side. I could not think of anyone who could help me come out of this state, but another autism mom. And then, in my mind, all my other mom friends came too. They gathered around me silently, putting their calming hands on my shoulders and my back.

Then I thought about all the mothers around the world, facing the same difficulties that I do, every day. I thought about all the different languages those mothers must be speaking. And about how all of our kids experience the same challenge, "speak" the same language. All they must be saying is "This is so hard for me, Mommy, please be with me." How these children are all united in some way. United, yet still fighting their way into our world.

I opened my eyes to me and Dan by ourselves, surrounded by the pure-white-snow in our back-yard. I felt a warm light coming from inside of me and then I knew that I was not alone. And Dan wasn't alone either. I looked up at the top of the trees surrounding our backyard and I saw rays of sunshine coming through the naked branches. I looked down and I saw that Dan had stopped crying. He finally calmed down.

Was it the swing that did that? Was it the fact that my thoughts carried me to a calmer place? As soon as we both regained our peace I started to feel the cold. My feet were frozen and so were my hands. I looked down and saw the mud on my shirt. I looked up again, and I saw a smile on Dan's face. That was all I needed. I didn't mind being in the mud forever if I could see this smile.

I thought about how most of the time, at this point in my life, I felt like autism for me was no longer about ego. It was not about wanting my child to be like everyone else. I was not holding onto all the dreams that he will be a doctor or a lawyer. It was not that. It was about this suffering and pain. All I wanted was that he would not suffer. Was that too much to ask, to achieve happiness?

But then there was this "other" mom inside of me. The one who was not ready to give up just yet. The one who, every time he reaches a point of calmness, was trying to push further. To see what more she could do in order to teach him. So he would get ahead. This "other mom" wanted to achieve not only happiness, but also success.

Could there be a way to achieve both happiness and success in the face of autism?

***

My name is Shirley and I'm an autism mom. After my son Dan was diagnosed with autism, I felt alone and isolated, as if cast into a different universe. The autism world was intimidating and scary, and I refused to be part of it. I was desperately longing to return to the life I had before.

Countless encounters with doctors, teachers, and specialists broke my otherwise optimistic spirit. Yet I refused to accept that there is no solution at all! Eventually my search lead me to an autistic spiritual healer – yes, you read that correctly – who helped me understand that parents are the primary healers of their autistic children, by being their channel to the world. I had to clean that channel in order for Dan to be able to connect with us, be a part of our universe.

When I first started to work with Joseph, my autistic spiritual healer, he explained that autism is a language that most people cannot understand. Joseph promised to teach me how to "speak" the right language with Dan.

What I didn't know at the time was that while I would be doing everything I possibly could in order to heal Dan, he would eventually heal me as well. The new understandings I acquired on my journey ended up changing both of our worlds.

I hope that you will enjoy my story, find inspiration and become empowered.

THE CALL

October 2006

My son Dan was diagnosed with autism when he was three years old.

"Diagnosed": What a cold and technical word to describe what a child and his parents go through during this unbearable time in the child's life. What we have gone through.

It started with a phone call from Dan's preschool teacher. It was a month after Dan started attending that preschool. We were still new in town. We moved to Connecticut from New York City when my husband Alex was offered a visiting professorship at Yale Law School. We were expecting our second baby, so I had not replaced my position as an attorney at a New York City firm just yet.

My parents were visiting from Israel, where I am originally from, and I was strolling with them around downtown enjoying the foliage that my mother loves so much. The trees created a canopy over our heads, with fiery red and bright yellow leaves falling off around us, creating their own little dance in the light breeze.

I heard my phone ring and I pulled it out of my purse nonchalantly while still talking to my dad, thinking it must be Alex calling to make lunch plans. As soon as I recognized the school's telephone number on the screen, the ring seemed to have turned into an alarm.

The teacher's voice was quiet and serious. She said, "Dan is OK now, but he had a very serious tantrum. He was completely beside himself. You should come pick him up now."

My parents and I rushed to the car. I came into the school by myself to find Dan playing happily, accompanied by a young teacher, who was not the one who called me.

"What happened?"

"I'm not sure. You should talk to Mrs. Stern."

While I was searching her face for a clue to what was going on, she avoided making eye contact, pretending to focus her attention on Dan. In the mean time, Dan kept himself busy climbing on the snack table. He was completely calm by this time and seemed very happy to see me. When he managed to get on the table despite the teacher's attempts to stop him, he stood there giggling as if telling her, "My mommy is here and I can do whatever I want."

At this point Dan was not talking yet. At age three, he had only a few words, most of them in Hebrew. When Dan was born in New York City, we consulted with the pediatrician on how to raise Dan as a bi-lingual child. She assured us that if we spoke only Hebrew to him at home, which was most natural to us as Israelis, "he will catch the English in no time when he goes to preschool."

While this may be the case for a typical child, in Dan's case, hearing only English at preschool made him more confused. His transition into preschool was much harder than that of the other kids.

On the way to the car, processing what had just happened, my heart sank. I worried that what we had been telling ourselves – that Dan is the youngest in the preschool and that he has a language barrier because of the Hebrew – were only part of the picture.

Arriving home, I raced to my bedroom to call Mrs. Stern, the director of the preschool.

Mrs. Stern was brief. She told me that she believed I needed to take Dan for a developmental evaluation. She gave me a telephone number of someone who was highly recommended. “I will call her myself, so she will get you in soon. She has an endless waiting list. With these things it is better sooner than later, you know?”

‘What things?’ I looked at the phone after she hung up.

That night when I was giving Dan his bath – which was not really a bath because he was afraid of water so our version of bath was him sitting in the empty bathtub while I shower him gently with a cup – I looked at his strong back and shoulders. His muscled body always seemed so adorable. He was my tall handsome boy with the dark brown hair and beautiful blue eyes that matched mine perfectly. But as I watched him bend forward to pick up a toy his shoulders seemed so sad, so powerless. He looked different to me that night.

Alex and I barely exchanged a word the entire evening. He sat at his side of the table pretending to work. The light from the lamp encircled him in the darkness of the living room, as if he was in his own bubble. My parents went to bed early. I fell asleep on the sofa watching TV.

EVALUATION

The next day I called the specialist. The evaluation process included a series of meetings and observations, at her clinic, at home and at Dan's school. Once the evaluation report was ready, we would meet with Mrs. Stern at the preschool to work out an action plan. I was not sure what that meant but I knew it wasn't good.

At the specialist's office, she asked us many questions about Dan's development. Dan met all his physical milestones in time: he crawled and sat and walked exactly when the books said he should. He said his first word when he was 6 months old. Yet he was not talking yet. 'What went wrong?' I thought to myself.

When she came to our house, Dan ran to the door to meet her. She brought a car toy that he was drawn to, and she tried to have him say 'go' before she pushed the button for the cars to go down the ramp. Dan was so excited he ran around in the room and then came back and tried to push the button himself. It was hard for him to pronounce the word 'go.' The specialist wouldn't budge, and after a few trials, Dan said 'o'. "That was good, right?" I turned to her, smiling from ear to ear. She didn't answer me and focused on working with Dan.

When the evaluation report was done, we came to meet with Mrs. Stern. Mrs. Stern was an older, tall, skeletal woman with thin straight grey hair down to her shoulders. She had tons of experience in child education, yet nothing about her said warmth or comfort.

The day of the meeting was rainy and gray. Alex and I could barely move that morning. We did everything so slowly. It was like a part of us already knew what was going to happen. Dan was his regular self. He ran around the apartment, coming to the table to grab a bite to eat and then continuing to run. When Alex and I were getting dressed, he climbed on top of the kitchen counter and played the way he played all the time: lifting a little person toy up towards the light and bringing it down.

We arrived at the meeting very late.

Mrs. Stern moved papers around and talked about the weather for a few minutes. This told us louder than words that we were about to receive bad news. But even though we thought we were prepared, we were in for a surprise.

“So we got the report,” she started, “The very long and thorough report.”

Oh, here it comes. I held Alex’s hand tightly.

“And all of us here at the school discussed it. And we believe Dan should not go here anymore.”

Alex and I looked at each other in shock.

“You mean we need to work on finding another school for next year?” Alex tried to soften the ax chop, “or for spring?”

“No, I mean now,” she said without a blink. “We think you need to pull him out immediately. He needs something completely different from what we can offer him here.”

We did not say anything so she continued.

"You remember when Dan had his first tantrum, six weeks ago?" she looked at me, "You asked the teacher if you should be worried." She paused for a minute and then said, "I am telling you that you need to be *very* worried."

My head dropped down and I closed my eyes. I braced myself so I would not punch her for labeling my child as damaged and for slamming the door in my face.

During the next few minutes all I could do was stare at my belly while playing with the edges of my red maternity blouse.

We all sat in silence for a while. The only sound in the room was the raindrops falling on the roof. Then I heard the kids playing in the background and something inside me wanted to run into the next room, grab Dan, leave, and never come back again. But I had to be rational. What good would it do?

I looked at Alex, my tall handsome husband with his strong shoulders. He was older than me and always knew what to do in any situation. He was so smart. I searched for his wise blue eyes, seeking comfort. He was bending his head down, looking completely helpless.

"You've got to give us time here. We've got to figure out a plan," he finally said.

Mrs. Stern shook her head. "It will not do Dan any good to be here."

"It will not do him any good to stay at home either."

While she was still considering it, I realized, that no matter what her decision was, I needed to figure out a plan, fast.

I took a big breath in, looked straight into her eyes and asked, "Where do I begin looking?"

Mrs. Stern arranged for us to meet yet another autism expert, to help us figure out the big question: what is the right program for Dan.

When we came to meet Dr. Expert, we realized how little we knew about our child and how little doctors knew about solutions for him.

While we were talking to the doctor, Dan was playing with a little person doll, lifting it into the air, and bringing it down, as if imitating an elevator. He was fidgeting and smiling the whole time. While Alex and I thought he was playing happily, Dr. Expert repeatedly touched Dan's shoulder and said, "It's OK, it's OK." He understood that Dan was "stimming," a professional term for self-stimulating. Dan's constant movement stemmed from his brain's necessity for it.

All in all, that meeting was disappointing. We were looking for a solution to our biggest dilemma: where exactly should Dan go for school? We wanted a prescription. All Dr. Expert could do was explain the different options: typical preschool with a professional shadowing Dan and helping him, "and good people are very hard to find, as well as typical schools who would let you do that"; Special needs school that would give Dan quality services, "and the problem there is that Dan won't have typical kids around him as role models"; and then you had public schools programs, that combine the typical peers factor with professional services, "but there are not many good programs and you need to live in that district in order to participate."

"How is the program in our town?" Alex asked.

The doctor shook his head. "You could check out the nearby towns. Some people move or get rentals in a different town so their kids can attend school there. Don't wait too long, though.

The best time for therapy is between ages two and five. That's when the brain is still forming. They call it 'the window'."

This was the first time we heard that autism parents have to figure everything out on their own, and that there's a deadline.

I hit the road and went to visit all the schools around our town, private and public. The foliage was gone and the view of naked trees and white snowy ground accompanied me as I travelled. Every morning, first thing after I dropped Dan off at school, I would go see a different school and meet with the director.

Dropping Dan off at preschool was hard. It was devastating to keep sending him there, knowing that the teachers did not know how to handle him. Most mornings Dan would not let me leave the school, holding onto me, crying and screaming. Yet at times he was happy to go there, running down the stairs and finding a toy to play with. That made it very clear to me that Dan did not share any of our worries. He did not understand any of it.

I, on the other hand, noticed each sign of the teachers' change of attitude. One morning when

I brought Dan to school, I saw his teacher – the same one who kept telling me how much she loved him — make a face and comment to another teacher about how Dan was running around and flapping his arms. She did not know I was still there. Dan had a hard time with the noise and the closeness of the kids, and he would compensate with this kind of behavior. That was another manifestation of that "stimming" we have just learned about. "What's with that?" was the expression on the teacher's face. They did not even try to understand him.

It broke my heart. It made me want to find a great school for Dan. A place that would have the key to make him better. A magical place where people would understand him.

While on the practical level it seemed like I was doing OK - focusing my energy on finding a school - on the emotional level things were different.

The time of getting a diagnosis of autism for your child is a very lonely one. When someone gets sick, people show their support: they bring food, they offer their help. When people hear someone has autism, they don't know how to help. Eventually, they just disappear.

At some point, I felt completely isolated. We had just moved to this town, and I had begun making friends, most of them were parents from Dan's preschool. But now he was setting off on a different path, and Alex and I felt like we were cast out.

There was no one I could take Dan to meet. There was no place I could take him to do anything. While in New York City we would take the stroller to Central Park or go to the few museums Dan knew and was used to, we couldn't do any of that in our new town. Here you had to drive everywhere. All the places were unfamiliar and Dan would not go in. He would show his protest by screaming and trying to escape from the stroller and run. Even a trip to the grocery store was a challenge. Overwhelmed by the bright lights and noise, Dan would scream or run and bang his head. After a few trials, we gave up and stopped taking him. One of us would go while the other stayed home with Dan.

While Alex went to work and had the chance to experience another reality, I spent my days at home with Dan. During those days, Dan would do one of two things: play with two pieces of puzzle, sliding them on the kitchen floor like sliding doors and hum; or play with a person toy lifting it up and bringing it down while sitting on the kitchen counter. I, on the other hand, sank into Sudoku puzzles. Most of the day, we were home doing exactly that for hours.

One night I had a dream. I was at my grandparents' apartment and my late grandfather was with me on the porch. I had called him and he came to see me. 'Help,' I said to him. Sitting on his favorite chair, he turned his body towards the street and called out. I couldn't hear his voice, yet I could tell that he was calling out for help. Within seconds the house started to fill up with old souls, like my grandpa. They were white, almost transparent. They all gathered. To help me.

I woke up feeling uplifted. And then reality dawned on me and my heart sank.

NEW FRIEND

January 2007

One day at the pediatrician's office I had a good surprise. I made a new friend. I met her in the waiting room. She was tall with long curly hair, like me. She came with a baby boy. I came with Dan. Both kids had ear infections. I heard her speak to her baby in Hebrew and when she and I started talking, I quickly learned she was also new in town. Her family had just moved here from Israel.

A few minutes into the conversation, my new Israeli friend Dalia invited us over to her house for dinner. We exchanged telephone numbers and she called me that same night.

"Is it OK if I talk to you like one autism mom to another?"

"Uh, OK," I said, thinking that I hadn't said anything to her about Dan yet. She must have picked up on it herself, seeing him in the waiting room.

"My daughter Nili is just a tiny little bit on the autism spectrum. She is going to be five in May."

From the moment Dalia got my "permission" to talk about autism, that's the only thing she talked about for the whole hour of our conversation. Her daughter was almost two years older than Dan, and I had just been taking my first steps and had almost no knowledge at the time, so I mostly listened.

When we hung up the phone I was in a complete panic. Alex looked up at me from his spot at the dining table. I had been sitting frozen on the sofa.

"What has she been telling you for the past hour?"

"It's terrible. She is friendly and open and warm, but the only thing we talked about for the whole hour was her daughter's autism. What therapy she was doing for her; what she had to do to find the right school; what kind of evaluations they were doing; what kind of evaluations they were going to do next; how hard autism is for Nili, and how hard it is for their family, especially

Dalia. She says raising a child with autism is like raising ten kids!"

I pulled the red blanket from the sofa and tightened it around myself.

In the following phone conversation it became absolutely clear that I had just found myself not only a friend, but also an expert on autism. Dalia had studied this field inside and out and knew everything there was to know. Yet, she did not stop at studying it. She was living it. It was scary, but at the same time I was fascinated.

When it was time to go to Dalia's house for dinner, I was very excited. More than six years after leaving Israel for the U.S., my joy at meeting new Israeli friends only grew with time.

We walked into their warm apartment and shook the snowflakes off of our coats. I took off my shoes and Alex helped Dan take his boots and coat off. As I walked into the living room I noticed the appetizing smells. Being seven months pregnant, I was always hungry, so I may not have been the best judge, but then Alex noticed too and complimented Dalia.

"This is my husband, Ethan, and his mom, Sarah, she is visiting us now from Israel." I shook Ethan's hand and then his mom's.

Alex started talking to Ethan about his new job as a researcher that had brought them to the U.S. It seemed like the two of them immediately bonded.

"Come with me," Dalia took my hand, "the kids are in the back." I took Dan's hand and we followed her. My heart was beating fast. It was my first time meeting a child with autism. "Special needs," is what Dalia kept on calling it, forgetting she had already used the "A" word in our first conversation.

We entered a room filled with so many toys there was barely a spot to place our feet. Nili was jumping on the bed singing in Hebrew and her baby brother was sitting on the floor throwing stuffed animals at her, to both of their delight. When Dan entered and saw Nili his eyes widened. He let go of my hand, ran to the bed and tried to climb on it to join her. He was too little to get onto the bed by himself. He looked at me and pointed at Nili. I picked him up and placed him next to her and they both bounced on the bed, she kept singing and he was squealing in delight.

Seeing Dan react this way to a new place filled with new people was amazing. Usually when we came to new places he would cling to me, or worse, try to run away. Alex and I believed that Dan was a good barometer of places and people. If he did not like a place, there was usually a reason. Once we went to visit a new friend, and he refused to go into the house. Soon after that, I learned that the husband was very ill and the couple was on their way to a nasty divorce. It was like he could sense the bad energy in that house. But that evening at Dalia's house, Dan was having a blast.

At the dinner table, all conversation was about autism. Ethan's mom was a psychologist who specialized in children and it seemed that all she and Dalia had been talking about was autism.

I examined Nili while nobody noticed and to me she looked fine! Her eye contact was brief, yes. One of the first things that come up with regards to autistic children is lack of eye contact. I could see hers was not perfect, but it seemed OK to me. And she was talking! She even spoke both Hebrew and English fluently. I was impressed. I didn't know at the time that although usually one of the first signs of autism is delay in speech, kids who *do* talk can have autism too.

Dan was sitting next to Nili and after eating a few bites he wanted to go back to playing. “Uh... Uh...” he said, pulling on Nili’s sleeve.

“Say Ni-li,” I said to him. “Ni... Ni... Ni...” I said and touched his chin softly like I saw our speech therapist doing at home.

When Nili finally joined him, they happily went back to bouncing on her bed.

“What evaluations did you do for him?” Dalia asked as her gaze followed the kids leaving the table.

“We met with Dr. Expert. He is the head of the...”

“Biggest and most important research center in the world,” Dalia completed the sentence for me. “How did you get to meet him personally?”

“He is on the board of the preschool Dan used to go to. When they realized Dan couldn’t go there anymore...”

“They kicked Dan out? That’s terrible.”

"They did it to us at Nili's preschool in Israel," Ethan looked at me, smiling warmly. "Dalia has been dying to get Nili for an evaluation with Dr. Expert. The waiting list to get in is five years."

"We were quite disappointed with him, though," Alex said. "Because he could not even recommend a good program for Dan. Shirley has been driving around for weeks to find the right place."

"I know how you feel," Ethan smiled at me again, "Dalia sent me here four weeks before they arrived, so I could find the right program and then an apartment in the right town."

On the way home in the car Alex and I agreed that the evening was very nice.

"Dan had a great time, right?"

"Yes, it's been a while since I've seen him so happy."

"Ethan seems like a great guy."

"Yes, he is. I enjoyed talking to him."

"She's something, huh?"

"Just like you described her. Did you see their library? The only books they brought with them from Israel are books about autism. Ethan told me that's why they moved here in the first place."

"Do you think we're going to become like that too?"

"I hope not. I want to be able to talk about things other then my son's condition. There has to be a life beyond it."

We both sighed quietly.

And then I turned back to look at Dan in his car seat. I elbowed Alex so he could see too. Dan fell asleep with the biggest smile on his face. And then I knew that we were going to meet this family again for sure.

After that dinner, in the weeks left before my scheduled C-section, we spent a lot of time with Dalia's family. Dalia showered our family with invitations. She always planned fun activities for the weekend and we joined and had a great time. She was a bulldozer but the result was a good time for everyone. Dan responded very well to their company, which also made Alex and I want more.

The one thing that was not fun at all was that not only did Dalia go on about everything she was doing for Nili, she also felt a need to be involved with everything we were doing for Dan.

Dan has just started the new program and also started getting speech therapy at home. Alex and I were happy with our choices of both school and speech therapist and tried to put our minds at ease and concentrate on the arrival of the new baby.

NEW BABY

March 2007

Gali was born on a Friday afternoon. My mom came from Israel two days earlier and she was the one who stayed with Dan when Alex and I went to the hospital that morning for my scheduled C-section.

During the hours until the procedure, I was thinking about how ever since Dan was born, every conversation I had with Teresa, my energy healer from Israel, she kept on telling me I needed to let go.

"What do you mean?" I would ask. And she would say, "You are holding on too tightly. He is his own person. He is your son but his soul does not belong to you. Stop focusing all your energy on him. You have other things, other people, in your life. When you let go, everything will flow much more easily." She had been saying that long before trouble started with Dan.

I was still struggling to understand the concept of letting go and not sure what I was supposed to do. But I felt like the birth of the new baby was an opportunity. A birth is such a huge, positive experience. I could utilize the positive energy involved in it to help me. I planned a little ceremony.

At the hospital, when my doctor came to check on me, I asked her, “Could you please tell me before you cut the umbilical cord? I want to see the baby before you do that.”

“Sure,” my doctor said, smiling. “I can do that.”

Two hours later Gali was born. When the doctor got her out she showed her to me.

“Can you see her?” she asked, “It’s hard to hold her, she’s really slippery.”

Gali still had all the fluids on her. She was still attached to me. But even in this state I could sense the liveliness shining from her. I felt connected to something much bigger. My eyes watered and my heart longed towards this beautiful baby who was my daughter.

And then it was time. The doctor announced "I am about to cut the umbilical cord now."

I took a deep breath in and closed my eyes and prayed. "I am letting you go, beautiful baby. You are your own person. I love you and I will always be there for you. I'm your mom. Yet you are a person on your own and I respect that." Tears were running down my face. I felt like the world stopped and the sun, the moon and the stars were taking part in this ceremony with me. "Dan," I thought picturing his beautiful face with his blue eyes smiling at me, "I am letting you go too, my boy. You are my son and I am your mom. Yet I accept that you are your own person. I love you and I will always be there for you."

And that was it. My secret ceremony: an attempt to let go of Dan in a positive way. I prayed that this would work. That this would eventually help Dan.

And then the doctor cut the cord and I heard a piercing scream. My baby. Screaming. What a strong voice. And I suddenly remembered that Dan did not scream like this. Dan made a sound. But it was a much quieter one. And I also remembered that even then, at the New York hospital, I had been worried for a second. Because

I had a feeling it should be different. Chills came down my back and my heart stopped.

Because I *knew* that *she* was perfect.

And at the same time that *he* might not be.

Or those were my thoughts at the time.

When they let me hold her I was overcome with joy. She was so beautiful. It was like all the beauty of the world, all its happiness, was wrapped in this precious baby. I kissed her ears, and head and chest and held her tightly close to my body.

I was nervous about taking Gali home, though. When you have a child with autism, bringing a new baby home is even more complicated than usual, because you are never sure how much they understand.

"You know Dan," I would say to him every day before the baby came, "soon you're going to have a little sister. She is going to be tiny at first, and then she'll grow up and learn how to play and she'll be your friend."

Dan wouldn't say anything. He kept lying on the bed next to me, putting his head on my belly. Silent. I had no idea how much of this he really understood.

The day after the delivery, Dan came with Alex and my mom to see me in the hospital. I missed not seeing Dan, even for one day.

Dan came into the room. As soon as he saw me his face lit up with a big smile. He ran to my bed.

"Here you are, Mr. Dan," Alex lifted him up and placed him by my side.

"Oh I've missed you," I said, giving Dan a big squeeze, as much as my achy body would allow me.

The baby was sleeping on my other side. Dan pulled his body up gently and peeked at her. We all held our breath. Dan then looked at me and slowly reached his little hand towards her and touched her head softly. My eyes watered and I heard Alex breathing heavily next to me. My mom turned in search for the box of tissues. Dan did not say a word, but he made his feelings clear to us that day.

Two days later I came home with Gali. And then things were not so peaceful.

The first night, Gali woke up in her bassinet crying. Dan, who slept with us in the bed, between me and Alex, immediately sat up and started to cry too. I picked Gali up and attached her to me. She calmed down as soon as she started to nurse. Dan on the other hand was still screaming in what seemed to be fear. The baby fell back asleep as soon as she was done nursing. It took us much longer to calm Dan down.

During the day, things were a little better. Dan would play by himself in his room a lot, which drove my mom crazy. He had changed in the months since she last saw him. He was in a new school and now he had a new sister, two things that would stress out any kid, but it was more than that. It was as if since we started the evaluations and received the diagnosis, Dan had become more absorbed in his own world. More autistic.

I often hear that from parents. Their kids have difficulties and they go for an evaluation. After they get the diagnosis their kids look so much worse. Is it because the parents see things they were not aware of before? I think it is more than that. I believe once we parents know there is something "wrong," we expect our kids to behave in a certain way, and then they slide into that place. They become it. Like our expectation creates something in them on some level.

As for the children, I think they feel our anxiety. After a diagnosis our anxiety rockets. Once they feel that and they see their parents in this state, the most natural reaction is to hide in their own world. They see us looking at them differently. They hear what we are saying about them. It is so natural to focus on the problem and forget to see the child!

After Gali was born, we too were so focused on worrying that we did not see that Dan presented typical behaviors as well. He wanted Gali's toys. He would grab her blanket and a pacifier and go to my mom when I was nursing asking to be picked up. It seemed like he completely understood the picture.

One morning Dan climbed into Gali's bassinet and fell.

My mom was sitting next to me on the sofa while I was nursing and Alex was making coffee. We were talking about "the situation with Dan," just like we did a lot of the time. I was partially listening to them but mostly focused on Gali. She felt so warm snuggled in my lap. Her little eyes closed as she nursed. I caressed the side of her face gently with the tip of my finger. She was so soft and gentle.

Suddenly I heard a thud and then a scream.

My mom and Alex ran to our bedroom. It turned out that when we were all busy in the living room, Dan went to our bedroom and climbed into Gali's bassinet. The bassinet was not big enough to carry his weight and he fell and hurt himself.

I was the only one who could not go there, because Gali was still nursing. I could hear their hysterical voices. My mom ran to get our first aid kit and I could hear Alex singing to Dan. It was the singing he would do when he was trying to calm Dan down but even more to calm himself.

I could tell Dan was bleeding. And so was my heart. Because I could not be there for him. Because I had a new baby who was taking his place.

Then I remembered a conversation I had with my doctor a few weeks before the delivery. I was sad that day, as I often was following the diagnosis. I told her I felt bad that the new baby would take Dan's place, especially when he needed me the most.

"Do you have siblings?" she asked.

"Yes, two sisters."

"And how do you feel about them?"

I started bawling. "I cannot see my life without them," I mumbled between the tears.

"So why do you think Dan would feel differently?"

Two weeks after I had Gali, the days and nights were hectic and very tough for us all, but I had one especially rough day.

That day I decided to leave Gali at home with Alex and my mom for little while and take Dan to the playground, just the two of us. He was happy to come with me and wanted to wear the new rain boots that he received as a present from my friend. We went to his favorite park and I pushed him on the swing for a long time.

At some point, my breasts were aching and I noticed that Gali's feeding time was getting close. I wanted to go home, but Dan refused to get off the swing. He kicked and screamed. My body was in such pain, that I could not really make him. I was afraid his kicking would hit the C-section incision.

It was getting dark. When I finally managed to get Dan out of the swing, he refused to walk. Those stupid new boots were too big for him. Why did I let him wear them in the first place? So I found myself with a screaming 3 year old stuck by the swings, with just the two of us left in the playground. I got dizzy so I had to sit down. The benches were a few steps from the swing, so it looked like Dan was by himself. It was getting darker and a group of people passing by looked at Dan with worry. I got up and walked to him, pain and all. I was afraid someone would grab him and run. I tried to explain to him that we had to go back home and that I could not pick him up and carry him. He refused to come. I finally picked him up and carried him to the car.

THE MIRROR PRINCIPLE

April 2007

On one of those stressful days I called my healer Teresa. I told her about my new friend, and she explained to me that Dalia was my mirror. "That is why she came into your life."

By that time, I have learned that Teresa never says anything to me unless it was important. Teresa became a significant part of my life after she healed me from migraines when I was 25 years old.

***

When I first heard about Teresa's healing practice, in November 1998, I had about three very bad migraines a week. I remember how I used to lie in bed, and picture the paramedics arriving in an ambulance to put me to sleep. It was that bad.

A friend who also suffered from migraines told me how after he went to see Teresa, he had a whole week free of migraines. He could not describe exactly what she was doing during therapy, only that it was "some kind of energy healing." She did not even touch him.

I could not believe it: A whole week free of pain. I had to try it. I told my friend, "I don't care if she sings and waves feathers around me." I called and made an appointment right then and there.

I arrived at a small house surrounded by a beautiful garden. Large trees were mixed with flowers all around me. I followed the pathway to the door, inhaling the enchanting scent of the roses from the bushes on both sides of me. I knocked on the door. I could hear two dogs barking. "Quiet, already!" I heard someone say and then she opened the door.

She was a tiny, beautiful woman. Wearing high-heeled shoes, her head almost reached my shoulders. She wore jeans and a flower print buttoned shirt and her long flowing curly hair was flying in every direction when she tried to smile and greet me, and move her dogs out of the way at the same time.

She sat me down in the living room and gave me a glass of water. The dogs rested in her lap, quietly. She looked at me with anticipation. I told her why I came and she said: “Come with me. Let’s check you out.” I followed her into the other room. It was a small room with a treatment bed in the center. The air was filled with the scents of herbs and aromatic oils.

“Lie down on your back, please,” she pointed at the bed. “Take off your jewelry and loosen your belt and bra. And next time please do not wear black. It might attract the wrong energies.”

I hesitated for a minute but then laid on the bed. “A week free of migraines,” I reminded myself.

I could hear music coming from the other room. It was soft voices singing. I closed my eyes in the dark and let the scents around me and the blissful music calm my body. I felt very relaxed. I closed my eyes and I saw bright colors. Like someone was gently pouring glowing paint in the air above me.

Teresa entered the room and stood behind my head. She put her hands above my forehead without touching me.

"Do you feel anything?"

"Warmth."

"Aha," she said. I could tell she was nodding in the dark room.

She stayed at my head for a while and then she went over my whole body slowly, staying longer over different parts of it.

I let myself sink into the relaxing feeling. When Teresa was performing the healing my mind was at ease. The bright colors turned into visions.

I was by myself in an empty white place, surrounded by fluffy white clouds. When the clouds shifted a little, I noticed that I was standing at the bottom of a marble white stairway. Someone must have signaled me to come up because I started climbing the steps.

Then I saw an ancient city from above. I was flying above its buildings, churches and turrets, seeing people walking the narrow streets looking small from the air.

On another one, I was little, very close to the ground, and was running in a blossoming sun washed garden, my little feet stamping on the soft light green grass and the dandelions and daisies.

When we sat down after the treatment, Teresa asked me what I have seen. I told her about the visions.

"They were so clear, like I was there. The colors had such vivid aliveness to them too."

"This is how colors are in the spiritual world. They're the same colors people see in their dreams, if they're lucky. The fact that you could see it here shows me that you are a very special soul. You can be a healer yourself one day if you choose to be."

I did not make much of it at the time, yet I kept coming for treatments. After that first appointment, I began feeling much better. After a few more weeks, my migraines were gone.

***

On the phone call, when I was telling Teresa about Dalia she asked patiently, "What bothers you about her?"

"I hate that she is so obsessed with the girl and her 'situation' all the time, like nothing else in life matters. I hate that she compares her girl to Dan. I hate that when Dan is doing well she always says something mean, like she is jealous, and when he is doing poorly she has that look of 'I told you so.' It's like she is doing everything she can to make me see how bad this is. How bad this is for me! I hate that she compares what the doctor said about her daughter with what he said about Dan. And worst of all, I hate that she is constantly on this rollercoaster of one minute saying 'it will be OK' and the next minute being madly worried!"

Teresa did not say anything for a while, letting me think about what I'd just said and waiting to see whether I had reached the answer on my own.

"She is just showing you what *you* are doing. I told you already that every thing and every person who comes to our lives is here to show us something. You can learn something from your professors, teachers, your kids, someone you meet in an elevator. You just need to listen and the universe will give you answers.

"This case with your friend is easy. She came to you at this significant time in your life. She is very much like you. This is why you connected so easily. But because she has a 'lesson' for you, you need to listen and be careful at the same time, because you may end up getting hurt. Enjoy the good things she brings and avoid the negative as much as you can. If the negative in this relationship is greater than the positive, stay away."

We were both quiet for a minute.

"And, Shirley," Teresa added with that special voice of hers that always tells me there is a 'message' in it for me, "Let go! Look at your friend and see what I mean."

I followed Teresa's advice and weighed the balance. At this point the friendship was still more positive than negative for me and for our family.

Dan still had such a good time when we would go to their house. I would leave Gali with our wonderful doula and go there in the afternoon. It was a good opportunity for Dan to get some time with me without the baby and for me to get a few hours without the stress of being alone with the two of them.

One afternoon when we parked at their apartment complex, Dan said "Nili."

There was more to come. One night when all of our family went there for dinner, they put Nili's baby brother Sam to bed. Dan was playing so he hadn't noticed. At some point he noticed the baby was missing. He started running around the apartment looking for him calling, "Sam, Sam!" Alex and I felt very encouraged that night, seeing Dan use his words and care so much.

FINDING A PROGRAM

May 2007

After we parted ways with Fantasy School, the preschool that sent Dan and us on a new path, we were referred to a speech therapist named Tova. She would come to our house to work with Dan. Tova became a great resource for us. She was a very warm woman, who was always happy to work with Dan and he was always happy to see her.

However, the first time she came to work with Dan, he wouldn't cooperate. He ran around his room, giggling. As soon as Tova tried to engage him, even get close to him, he screamed. I rushed into the room and hugged him.

"It's OK, Dan," I said, "Tova just wants to play with you."

Tova examined my face for a minute.

"You know, there are two ways we could do this. The first is for me to teach you the technique so you and Alex can work with Dan. The second is for me to actually work with him. I honestly think it should be both. He will scream at first because he's not used to anyone trying to make him talk. But that doesn't mean he's in pain. He is expressing his protest. That's all."

She had already figured me out. I could not stand Dan being unhappy. I left the room and let her continue.

Tova also went to observe Dan at school. After the visit, we sat and talked. She told me about a typical daycare she knew, Happy Kids, that she thought would be a better fit for Dan.

I remembered that this was one of the three options Dr. Expert described to us, to have Dan in a typical school. He had explained the importance of typical peers as role models.

It was May. Five months after the diagnosis. Three months after Dan started the public preschool and a month before Dan's program went into its summer break.

According to Tova, Happy Kids had included children with special needs in the past and it worked well for everyone. She spoke to the director and told me to go see her with Dan. "Just go check it out. See what you think."

Dan and I went early in the morning. It was important we did it that way, because then there were fewer kids, and the place was quiet and less overwhelming for Dan.

Alma, the director of Happy Kids, a sweet lady with a big smile, welcomed us at the door, and took us into the daycare space. I loved the way it was designed, with big windows looking out to a spacious yard. She took us to the back room where they had fish and turtles and lots of toys. One of the teachers came to play with Dan. She knew how to sign. They were teaching the children how to sign on a regular basis there. Sign language is one of the methods that helps some kids with autism communicate.

Dan was happy to be there and started playing with the teacher immediately. One of the kids arrived early and came to see Dan. Alma told him Dan was visiting and he went and got something he wanted to show him. He was one of those kids who would not stop talking and he did not care much that Dan was not talking back. He kept on showing him the magnifying glass he was holding. Eventually Dan took an interest in that and started looking at the boy, shyly. When the short visit was done Dan did not want to leave.

Later that day Alma called me. She told me how impressed she was with Dan. She also told me that they had had children with special needs at Happy Kids in the past, and that both those kids and the other kids in the daycare enjoyed and learned from the experience. She asked if I was willing to let Dan try Happy Kids.

"If we did it over the summer, you could still keep the placement at Public Preschool. If it works out, Dan could move to Happy Kids for the next school year, and if it doesn't, for reasons I can't see, Dan could go back to the public preschool once the year started, in September. This way you have nothing to lose."

I could not believe it. A typical daycare was going to accept Dan. Autism and all. Both Alma and Tova believed he would be successful there.

Dan started that summer. He had a great time. On his first day he befriended Carol, one of the teachers who spoke some Hebrew, and Alma quickly put Carol in charge of Dan's group of kids.

One older boy "adopted" Dan and helped him play with the other kids. Soon Dan learned how to nap there and he started staying the whole day. The first few days, even with all the good stories, Alex and I were sitting by the phone, waiting for them to call us to come pick Dan up. It could not be, could it? And then after Dan had been there for three weeks, the teachers had a meeting with the director, to see how everybody felt about Dan staying for the coming school year. I did not know when they were going to do it, but one day Alma called and asked if I could come in for a talk.

What a flashback I had. I had been called to talk to directors before. I know exactly what happens at those talks, and how it all ends. Just give it to me straight, I thought.

Alma sat me down and told me there had been a meeting and all of the teachers felt that Dan should definitely stay.

"He does not belong in special education," she said. "You should of course continue with the speech therapy. You can even do it during his school day. We can give you a room for that if you need it."

I could not believe my ears. My heart was about to burst. My son, Dan, the one with autism, was just invited to attend a typical daycare. They thought he could do well and they thought it was the right place for him. I was in heaven.

Alma was an administrator with lots of experience. But there was a big difference between Alma and Mrs. Stern, who had asked Dan to leave her preschool. Alma saw things differently. She understood education differently.

Alma was the reason I started to trust the world again. After all this time of feeling rejected and having no hope as to how things were going to turn out for Dan, I started regaining my hopefulness. She awakened my optimism.

The first few months were great. Dan had a good time at school. The children were very accepting. Dan started following them and it seemed that he was learning from them. One day I came to pick him up and saw him running outside with the whole group. My eyes started to water. My son, Dan, was playing with typical kids and enjoying it.

While Dan was at school, I could spend undistracted time with Gali. That summer gave me the perfect combination. I had quality time with her and at the same time I knew Dan was having a great experience. He was happy.

FEELING GUILTY

September 2007

When Gali turned six months old, I placed her at Happy Kids. It was actually thanks to Dan's going there that Gali was bumped up the long waiting list and was offered the spot.

Naturally, I didn't want to send Gali to daycare so early. She was so young. But as a parent to a child with autism, you are always worried about what you've done wrong. I knew by now that if I had sent Dan to a daycare when he was a baby, instead of keeping him home with a Hebrew-speaking nanny while I went back to work at the law firm, the daycare teachers would have detected the autism earlier than we did. Having him home with his wonderful nanny made him and us very happy, but perhaps if he was around other babies and compared to them, we would have seen things earlier and helped him sooner.

So from that guilt over messing up Dan's development, I sent Gali to daycare early.

I believe that feeling guilty is a natural part of motherhood. However, when you have a child with autism, it is magnified. Faced with so many kinds of programs, therapies and treatments, you always feel like you want to try and do more. When a treatment works, you feel guilty about not trying it earlier. When a treatment fails, you feel guilty for putting your child and your family through it.

My own feelings of guilt went in all different directions. I especially wondered why I hadn't stepped out of denial sooner.

Another thought that would not leave my mind was, what if I did this to him somehow? What if I drank or ate something while I was pregnant? What if when he was a baby I mistreated him somehow? Maybe I am still doing something wrong now!

If one of the pharmaceutical companies invents a pill to treat that, a pill that takes away guilt, they are guaranteed to make millions. Think of all the energy we spend on the question "why did I do this?" and "what if I had done that?" If only we could take a pill and forget about it, we could go on with our lives and use that energy for better things.

Gali was the one who helped heal my feelings of guilt. She grew so fast and became such a loving and social creature. I had the time of my life with her. I realized that I treated her the same way I had treated Dan. And here she was, completely autism-free. It was not me! I did not cause any part of Dan's autism. It just happened. And I got this wonderful gift in the form of a beautiful daughter to show me that.

When I separated from my guilt, it got me thinking. The other side of guilt feelings is control. Because if I caused my child's autism then I can do something to take it away, right? When I was holding on to the guilt I was also holding on to the illusion of being able to fix Dan's autism. Perhaps separating from the guilt feelings is not as simple as I thought. Because then you have to separate from the idea that you have control over what is happening to your child.

LEARNING A NEW HEALING METHOD

October 2007

When Gali started going to daycare at Happy Kids, I had an opportunity to learn a new healing method, Bach Flowers Therapy. My friend from New York attended a lecture about it and was completely fascinated. She knew about my interest in natural healing and spiritual therapies, and when she heard that Tamara, the speaker, was from Connecticut, she got all excited. She sent me her information.

I went on the website and got goose bumps. I decided immediately that this method was something I wanted to learn about. It was based on the mind-body connection.

I called Tamara and made a time to come see her. When we met we connected immediately. We both spoke the same "spiritual language." I told her about my limited schedule, and she came up with a series of one-on-one classes that I could take while the kids were at daycare.

During my first class, I learned that Bach Flowers are a natural remedy that works on balancing our emotional channels. The method was based on the understanding that what we experience as physical pain is an expression of our mind or our soul telling us that something is not balanced. The role of a Bach Flower therapist is to find what's not balanced and provide the right flower essence for that emotional state. Naturally, Bach Flower Remedies work for emotional challenges as well as they do for physical challenges.

I learned how each of the 38 Bach Flowers essences — which were produced from actual trees, plants and flowers — could balance a certain element in a person's emotional state. Tamara categorized the essences into groups so it would be easier to understand. There were essences to help with balancing fears and anger, essences for boosting self-confidence and optimism, and an essence for grounding, which I immediately took an interest in.

After my third class, my teacher prepared a little bottle of Bach Flowers for me to take. As soon as I started taking my Bach flowers essence, I could feel the effect on myself. First of all I could think more clearly. I could concentrate and see things in my life for what they truly were. I also felt calmer and happier.

Tamara gave me the assignment to give some Bach Flowers remedies to Alex. He was tired all the time and it was obvious to me that his fatigue resulted from something other than lack of sleep, commuting and working long hours. I knew the same was true for other frustrations he was experiencing in his professional world. They were reflections of the much bigger frustration. The biggest: autism.

Alex also felt much better after he took the Bach flowers.

And then I asked my teacher if I could give some to Dan.

"Of course!" her face lit with excitement. "From what you have told me, I feel that he is very sensitive. He is also exposed to energies. There is a really good essence for that. It provides an energetic shield to the person who takes it. The other essence I would add for him is one that helps a person let go of the past."

Two days after I started giving Dan his Bach Flowers remedy, he gave up his blanket and his pacifier. I could not believe my eyes. The "blanket" was a rag by now. It was the remains of Dan's favorite blanket that we got him when he was born. Dan would carry that "blanket" everywhere and would have a pacifier in his mouth all day long. After he took the Bach Flowers for two days, he put both items away and did not even look for them ever again.

That same week, when I came to pick Dan up from Happy Kids, Carol, his teacher said, "What happened to Dan this week? It's like he's filled with light."

I was delighted to have found one more way to help my boy. I finished my studies and became a Bach Flowers therapist. Later on I organized a local workshop about healing and started seeing clients. My dream became to help children like Dan.

BIG BUMP IN THE ROAD

December 2007

And then things stopped working at Happy Kids. It was in the late fall when Alma the director called me and told me that Dan could no longer stay for nap. It would take him a long time to fall asleep, and he had to have his favorite teacher with him the whole time, and they could not do that anymore. I had to pick him up now at 1 instead of 4:30.

At about the same time, Alex told me that he felt like Dan was "stuck." He did not see him progress the way he had expected and it worried him.

I made an appointment for us to see a child psychologist recommended by our pediatrician. Dan had to go through yet another round of evaluations. Another round of being asked to do things he cannot do. We had to go through another round of slaps in our faces, telling us how bad things actually are.

We got all of that, and more. We were in for an unpleasant surprise. When this experienced woman, the child psychologist, sat us down for the final talk, she told us we were doing it all wrong.

"Happy Kids is not the right program for your son. When I was there he was walking around flapping his arms and nobody stopped him. I wanted to simply grab them and explain it to them!

"Tova, your speech therapist, is not such a good fit for Dan either. This is not the approach that he needs right now. Maybe it worked in the beginning, but not anymore, in my opinion."

"So what do you think he needs?" Alex asked her.

The psychologist's face lit up with joy. "I would like to see Dan in a program where they have strict one-on-one applied behavior analysis (ABA) kind therapy; Where they have structured play time with typical peers, supervised by professionals; and of course speech therapy and occupational therapy as much as possible."

"That sounds good. Where is this program?"

Although I was having a hard time accepting the psychologist's opinion that everything we were doing was wrong, I was happy that Alex was asking those questions. If that was what Dan needed, we should at least check it out.

"Well, see, that's the thing, there is no such program. You would have to come up with it by yourselves."

Alex looked at me. 'Here we go again,' said his eyes.

"There are some good public school programs but they keep on changing," she said. "Town X was golden until this year when their director moved to Town Y. So now Town Y will be great once she gets a hold on things, but that may take a while."

"So basically you are telling me that there is no way of *knowing* and this is all guess work anyway."

"Well… in a sense yes."

"Until we find the golden program, what *could* we do while Dan is at Happy Kids?"

"You need new therapists. You have to change his speech. You need more therapy that is tailored to his current needs. Behavioral therapy. I think he needs a full time special education program. If you want him to stay at Happy Kids, at least bring in help. Someone who would make sense of his day there."

OK, total reboot. That was what she said.

I had to go searching again.

I went back to the specialist who evaluated Dan in the beginning, to see if maybe now she was available to provide therapy. She was not, but she did refer me to someone she knew, and, as she put it: "Every time I see her work, I learn something new." I called that speech therapist and made a time to go see her.

Then I talked to Sydney, Dan's occupational therapist. Sydney was the only person who was a solid rock for me to lean on no matter what program Dan was at and no matter what was going on. She was a sweet soul and a gifted therapist.

At Dan's first session with Sydney, he was simply running around the clinic. There was no way she could engage him in anything. Sydney grabbed Dan's little body gently and pressed her fists onto his heels in an attempt to ground him. He calmed down immediately. She explained to me about energy centers in the body and I immediately knew we had found what we needed.

After two weeks of searching and reshuffling I thought I had reached a solution.

Dan started seeing the new speech therapist in the afternoons, after I picked him up from school at 1 pm, the new time. He would also see Sydney one day after school and on Saturdays. Also, Sydney would go to Dan's school in the mornings, to support him during the social activities that were challenging for him. In order to keep Dan's day as full and structured as possible, I brought him back to Happy Kids after his speech therapy. The other kids were already awake after nap and he got more time to play between three and five.

I figured that this way we covered it all. We implemented the new "prescription" given by the psychologist. The speech person was using behavioral methods. Sydney was using her regular magic, and by having Sydney go to school and support Dan, Dan's experience at Happy Kids was more meaningful for him. She helped the teacher set up the environment in a way that was helping Dan cope with his sensory overload. She would provide the deep pressure that Dan often needed for his body to function.

"See?" Sydney told me when I came with Dan to see her one of the Wednesday evenings, "once we moved this book cabinet here," she pointed at a picture she took, "Dan's area was more restricted and he was less bothered with that side of the room, which is always so noisy. This way he could concentrate on the project they were doing at his table. And he really had fun. I can tell that Dan really wants to participate. His body is just so overwhelmed because his brain processes information differently. It is a common mistake to think kids with autism do not *want* to play with other kids and participate in social activities. They *cannot* because it is painful for them."

The new plan seemed to be working really well for Dan in the first few weeks.

I did not want to admit it, even to myself, but it was very hard for me. Before this change, both kids were at the daycare for a full day. It was the time after I had completed my Bach Flowers Therapy course, and was taking the first steps towards creating my own practice. Now the schedule completely shifted. I would come to pick Dan at 1 pm, drive him to therapy, bring him back to school, and then pick him up together with Gali at 5 to face the evening activities with both kids.

More than the hardship of running around and dealing with transition issues all day long (children with autism have a hard time moving from one activity to another) was the emotional burden. There were two times a day that I had to pass by Gali's "baby room" to pick up Dan and bring him back. This involved a whole operation.

The first step was opening the door to a tiny crack and making eye contact with one of the teachers. She would then sign me if Gali was sleeping or up and playing. If she was in the nap room, I could openly walk by and go to Dan's "big kids" room. If she was up and playing, the teacher would nod her head in the direction of where Gali was. Most often in that situation I would kneel down and crawl the long hallway to Dan's room, while the teacher would make sure to have Gali's attention on her play and to block her view from where I was.

The second step was to bring Dan out without Gali noticing us. That was much harder, because Dan would take his time walking out.

He would find something on the wall to play with. He would look into the baby room. I would be sprinting the few feet until I reached the low wall that was separating the baby room from the hallway, and kneel behind it, and wait for Dan to come toward where I was so I could open the door for us to get out. Me crawling and him walking.

When I brought Dan back at 3 pm Gali was usually taking her nap so I could enjoy the privilege of walking in with my head up high.

It was a choice I made. I hated to do this, but I had to. Dan needed this. He needed me.

Blog Post from my website March 11, 2011:

GPS for Autism Treatment

Being an autism parent means lots of things. Like planning ahead. I mean really. Everything. You never know what will work and what won't so you have to be ready for everything. My friend Rena says you have to be like a chess player – plan three moves ahead. My friend Gretchen says you have to be like a colonel in a battlefield, because you never know where the next grenade will come from.

The biggest thing for me with autism is figuring out the healing journey of treatments and therapies. There are so many things out there: From the mainstream speech and occupational therapy to horses, music and the million alternative therapies. There are so many different diets and supplements.

Many times we started something and it looked like it was working very well. But then it stopped. And then sometimes things got worse!

I wish there was a GPS for therapy. Something that would help me figure out in real time whether something is working and what to expect soon. Like if whatever we are doing right now is working the device will say "keep straight!" And if it is working but we have to change something soon it will say "in 800 yards, turn right!" If something is about to completely fail or get worse my GPS will say "turn around when possible!"

And once we have done everything possible known to man and it actually all worked, the device will say what all of us autism parents long to hear: "You Have Reached Your Destination!"

LOOKING AT THE BODY

February 2008

That winter I came across a book about bio-medical treatments for autism, and how by implementing special diets and different supplements, many parents had managed to cure their children.

I decided to take Dan to a naturopathic doctor to pursue that path.

The doctor we went to see was a young, energetic woman. She was a friend of a friend. She had three young children of her own and I would see her with them at the playground sometimes on weekends. She would always pull out bags of healthy snacks for them. I remembered how watching those kids eat raw broccoli for a snack made me green with envy. We had brought potato chips to the park that day.

When we went to see her, she examined Dan's body, paying particular attention to his skin and nails. Then she filled out forms for a blood test and a urine test.

When the test results arrived, she told me that Dan was sensitive to gluten and casein, the protein found in dairy products. She advised that I put him on a gluten-free and casein-free diet. I had read enough autism books by that time to know that this was the popular diet for kids with autism, so I was not surprised, yet I had no idea how to actually do it.

"It's not that hard," she said when she saw the panic on my face.

Easy for her to say. Dan's diet at the time included mac & cheese, cookies, crackers, bagels dipped in syrup (yes!) and fruit. Fruit was the only thing that could still be included in the new prescribed diet. I had to find replacements for the rest.

"Start slowly," the doctor said. "Get familiarized with the different foods out there. Get him used to it gradually. Don't just take everything away from him at once, because then you'll fail to maintain the diet in the long run."

I went to the health food store straight after the appointment was over. If that was the diet that Dan needed in order to beat autism, I was up for the challenge. The first thing I noticed when I was walking the aisles of the store was how much more expensive everything was. Every package of gluten-free pasta cost three times more than the regular pasta. Every loaf of gluten-free bread cost twice more than the delicious gourmet bread we bought at our regular store.

I decided to replace everything I could in Dan's diet immediately. I bought the gluten-free bread and gluten-free pasta and gave them to Dan that day. To my surprise, he actually liked them. I bought new kinds of cookies, and he liked them too. That weekend I took away all the forbidden foods and served only the new foods, and Dan was fine with it. Alex made a face, of course, when the gluten-free pasta replaced the usual spaghetti, but I told him that I believed that Dan would not have to be on this diet for too long. After all, I read about children with autism who improved very quickly on these diets.

But then Monday came and it was time to go to preschool. At Happy Kids they served snacks to the kids in the mornings and the afternoons. They gave them Goldfish crackers, Cheerios and fruit. The only thing Dan could have of those was the fruit. But fruit doesn't keep a kid full for too long. Dan wanted the crackers. He was hungry. He also couldn't understand why all the kids were having them and he wasn't allowed.

But I decided to stick to my guns. I had read so many stories about kids who had recovered from autism after doing the diets, so I had to finish what I had started.

The preschool teachers followed my instructions. In those few weeks Dan got so skinny, but I refused to quit. One day when I came to pick him up I saw him eat sand out of the sandbox. Then I saw him grabbing and eating a cracker that one of the kids dropped to the floor.

And the worst part was that Dan started having abdominal pains, and his stools became watery and painful. That I could not take. It brought back too many memories of Dan at age two, when he became very sick.

***

This happened in December 2005, during a visit to the family in Israel. Dan caught a terrible stomach virus and was in severe pain for the remainder of the visit, three whole weeks. He was so miserable. We ended up cancelling all of our plans and staying at my parents' house the whole time. Instead of enjoying the company of our friends and family and the nice weather, all we wanted was to go back home to our tiny apartment in snowy, freezing New York City.

Dan could not retain anything he drank or ate. He would throw up and if we gave him water very slowly so he could keep it down, he would have clear, bursting diarrhea shortly after. He was in so much pain and there was nothing we could do to help. The skin on his bottom was one big burn. Whatever was coming out of there was so acidic it burned him. He could not stand to have the diaper on him so he lay naked on the bed and when he would throw up or have a diarrhea, we washed him and changed the pile of towels under him.

My parents witnessed this and could not believe their eyes. When we first arrived, Dan was happy. He would sing and play with them. But then the illness made Dan disappear. He was in such pain and misery.

The flight back to New York was a nightmare. Dan would not stop screaming. We had to put a diaper on him while we were on the airplane, and his burning skin hurt so much. Every time he had to go, we did our best to clean him so the residue would not continue to touch and burn his skin even more. We had a pile of very good creams provided by the Israeli doctors, but by this time his flesh was exposed so the creams could not provide comfort.

The crew on the plane tried to help us. "Is everything OK with him? Do you need us to find a doctor?" they kept asking. "No, there is nothing to be done," we said.

***

When we finally got home Dan was different.

The best way to explain the change in him after the illness is to tell you about how he was before.

Dan used to be a shy baby. During the summer of 2005, before we went on that visit to Israel, Dan finally made a best friend, Liam. This was a boy exactly Dan's age, 18 months at the time. Dan's nanny and Liam's mom saw each other at Central Park a few times. During those spontaneous meetings in the park, the boys started to play together on the playground.

Dan had to see them a few times before he fully opened up, but once he did it was pretty amazing to watch what happened. Liam was practically in love with Dan, and Dan simply blossomed in his presence. Dan would do funny things, and since Liam simply followed him wherever he went and did what he did, it was twice as fun. One day, Dan ran to a police car, hung himself on the open window, and started talking to the policemen. Liam followed, and hung himself onto the other window, and they were both standing there talking gibberish with the laughing policemen, to the delight of everyone around them watching.

Now you see, it was so hard for me to get a diagnosis of autism a year and a half after this. How could a child who initiates such games and tricks be autistic? I always thought autistic children sat in the corner all day by themselves.

Dan became the center of attention when he was without Liam, too. One Saturday morning he caused quite a scene again. He ran to his other "friend," the saxophone player. This was a guy who played in one of the jazz clubs in the city, and would come and spend his days in the park practicing, with his hat on the floor in front of him. Dan, who loved music, was fascinated with him. On that Saturday, Dan ran to him and started dancing to the music. This created such an attraction. Many people quickly surrounded the two of them. A group of tourists asked Alex if they could take pictures of Dan.

When we returned from Israel after Dan got sick, it took Alex and me a while to realize that something was different. At first, we were just happy to be back home, and hoping to leave the trauma behind us. All we wanted was to go back to the reality we had before we left. When Alex was teaching at the law school and I split my time between being with Dan and having some time for myself (at this point I had lost my legal job and was searching for a new one). Our weekly activities included trips to the park, children's museum, attending Dan's gym class and frequent play dates with Liam.

How precious is routine and how often we take it for granted.

Now Dan could not participate in any of the activities he had engaged in so naturally before. Even though he was no longer terribly sick, it seemed like he was never comfortable. We could not put our finger on exactly what went wrong.

As I was trying my hardest to return to our old routine, I bumped into obstacles left and right. Soon after we returned home I found out that Liam had already found another best friend. She was an Israeli girl who went to preschool. They would meet every day after she was done, and their play was different. She spoke fluently. She played the big kids' games. She colored and knew her ABCs. A whole different ball game from how Liam and Dan had played: running together and being silly.

At first Liam's mom tried to have us join them. The first time we came, Dan was chewing on the food toys. "You know they are not really supposed to do that at this age?" she said to me.

The next time we came, Dan was chewing on Liam's baseball bat. Liam wanted it too. I tried to take it from Dan, but he really hung onto it. Liam started to whine loudly, until his mom, who couldn't stand the noise, came over and took it from Dan. She simply pulled it out of his mouth. Dan was so upset and I could not calm him down, so we had to leave immediately. That was the last time we saw them. We were not invited again.

Each way I turned in an attempt to gain our routine back was blocked. Dan could not attend his gym class anymore. He would try to run out of the room all the time. All the activities he did with his nanny he could not do anymore. He would escape from the stroller and run toward the busy city street. He did not eat the same way anymore. He was restless all the time.

AWAKENING

March 2006

In the months that followed our return from Israel, it seemed like Dan never got over the horrible virus he had. He suffered from stomachaches constantly, and his stools were watery and would burn his bottom.

During that time a few things happened: I found a new legal job, we lost our beloved nanny after she had her own baby, and Dan started going to a new daycare, so I could go to work.

After just a few weeks of attending the day care, they asked us whether Dan had seen the doctor lately because they had some concerns. We contacted 'Early Interventions' and began a round of meetings and evaluations that stressed Alex and me out. However it all ended shortly after it started. Dan was too young, they said, for an official diagnosis.

Besides the behavioral concerns that the school raised, Dan was still very uncomfortable and sick a lot. I struggled to make sense of everything that was happening.

I was having lunch with a friend from work, Dana, and after I told her about my situation she suggested I talk to her mom. Dana's mom, Amelia, was the editor of a very big parents' magazine in Israel and had access to all the big doctors and experts. "She knows absolutely everyone and she would be happy to help. I will talk to her and let you know a good time for you to call her."

Two hours later she called me in my office. "Call her now! She is waiting for you by the phone." It was 4 pm New York time and 11 pm in Israel so I had to hurry. I ran to the closest meeting room and closed the door behind me.

The talk with Amelia opened my eyes. I told her about Dan being uncomfortable and I told her about the daycare people in New York who encouraged us to evaluate Dan for developmental delays.

"What is Dan saying? What is he doing?"

"He has about 5 words by now...." I said, assuming she meant how much talking Dan managed to do at age two and a half years.

"No," she stopped me, "what else is he saying? What kind of sounds does he make?"

"He is talking to us in Gibberish, and once I tried to imitate a few of his "words" and he was so happy he ran to me and hugged me."

"Shirley," she said, "you have a very special boy who sees things. He has the ability to connect to different times and places. People around you have a hard time understanding kids like him. They will look for a label to put on him because they are uncomfortable with things they do not understand. Do not let them scare you because all they are trying to do is fit Dan into the box they are familiar with. He is different but that is not a bad thing."

She asked me more questions: "How is he physically? Is he sick a lot?"

I told her about the stomach virus and how at that time he had experienced another version of it.

"Pain in the stomach is usually associated with fears. What might Dan be afraid of?"

I told her about all the changes we had been going through.

"You must help him with the pain. Get some lavender oil and rub it on his tummy in circles. Then picture black things leaving his stomach and flying away. These are the fears leaving him. After that he will feel much better."

I thanked Amelia and hung up the phone. Then I sat there for a while, digesting the things she had said to me. I was impressed with the way Amelia was thinking. Her approach was the closest I had ever heard to Teresa's way of thinking.

***

You see Teresa did not just heal me from my migraines. She was the first one to awaken my intuition. She did it by teaching me how to interpret my dreams. She believed that our dreams contained messages from our "higher-self," and once we learned to understand the messages, our dreams could guide us. Every time I came to see her for a healing session, we would sit down and Teresa would go over my dreams from the past week and interpret them for me, while teaching me how to do so myself.

I started receiving proof of the change in me shortly after we started this routine. I started to understand things in my life in a different, deeper way.

The first time I noticed it was in the winter of 1999. I was sitting in my apartment in Tel Aviv and studying for my finals. It was my last year in law school and I was on a job hunt. I had just finished an internship with an especially toxic partner at a law firm that specialized in real property transactions. I was looking for something completely different from that practice. A few days earlier, I had interviewed with a law firm I really liked. Their specialty was intellectual property. All three partners who interviewed me seemed like great people to work with.

While studying, suddenly a thought crossed my mind: "they are talking about me." And then an image of Mary, my friend from law school, came to my head. Seconds after that, the phone rang.

"You will not believe who is here for a meeting..." I heard Mary whispering, short of breath with excitement. Apparently, one of the partners from the firm I liked had been at Mary's firm for a meeting. She met him in the waiting room and told him she knew someone who interviewed with his firm. "I just managed to get out of there and come call you. He was questioning me about you forever!"

Soon after that I ended up getting the desired job. After a successful and exciting year of specializing in intellectual property, I furthered that opportunity, moving to New York to earn a masters degree in intellectual property law, and secure a job in a desired New York City law firm.

That winter of 1999 was the first time I was getting information about something that was happening somewhere else, without being there in real time. I had yet to learn to believe in myself, and follow my intuition.

***

Returning to New York in 2006, I left the office after ending the conversation with Amelia. On my way home I stopped at the Whole Foods store in Columbus Circle and I bought lavender oil.

That night, after Dan fell asleep, I decided to do what Amelia told me. While I was rubbing my hand on Dan's belly in circles something strange happened. It was like something told me to lift my hand. "This is how we do it, remember?" was what came to my mind. I lifted my hand over Dan's belly and did what I saw Teresa do so many times. I felt warmth coming out of Dan's belly into my hand. I knew something was happening, but was not sure what it was.

That night I dreamed that I was flying. I felt like I was lifting off of my body, I circled the ceiling of my bedroom, and then I left through the window and flew into the night sky.

The next day Dan woke up feeling well.

I was making coffee in the kitchen when I heard him going for a number two in his diaper. 'Oh no, here it comes,' I thought. Usually what followed was screaming because of the pain from the burning stool on his skin. This morning I heard nothing. I went to change him and he did not resist like always. His stool was fine and he behaved like he was pain free.

I did it!

MY HUSBAND ALEX

Aristotle said that you do not truly know a friend until you shared a peck of salt with them. When autism came to our lives, Alex and I began to share one.

Truthfully, Alex and I were not your typical couple to begin with. He is 15 years older than I, we both have been married once before, and Alex also has kids from his previous marriage.

We met during one of Alex's visits to New York City, when I was studying for my master's degree. Even with the age difference, we had a lot in common. We started a long distance relationship, which included spending hours on the phone and visits every few months, either me going to Israel or him coming to New York City.

With Alex, I was getting everything I always longed for in a relationship: someone with whom I could really talk, and who was truly focused on me. The time we spent together during the visits was relaxed. It was always just the two of us. This was different from the relationship I had with my first husband, who liked to be surrounded with friends all the time. Alex and I explored the city, enjoyed good restaurants, and could talk forever. Our relationship turned out to be the passionate love I was longing for.

We got married in Israel two years after we started dating. Dan was born in New York almost a year after we got married.

When Dan was fifteen months old Alex noticed that he was not making eye contact and would not respond to his name. At that time I did not suspect anything. Dan was playing well with his nanny and with me. He would look at books and play with toys.

I forgot all about Alex's remark during that beautiful summer of 2005 in the city, when Dan was eighteen months. Everything seemed to be alright.

And then Alex noticed something wrong, again. It was at Liam's birthday party. The party took place at Liam's music class' space, a tiny spot that was packed with colorful toys and musical instruments. We've never been there before. As soon as we walked in, Dan started running around the room. He was obviously over-stimulated, but we didn't know anything about that at the time.

While Liam was participating in lots of classes in addition to playing with Dan, there was only one class Dan was able to participate in. It was at My Gym, a kids' gym, with trampolines, ball pit and toys to climb on. When he was at a gym class, he never sat for the "circle time" part of the class. Since there was always at least one more child not sitting, I was not too worried. I would always joke about it with the other mom whose child was also not sitting, usually another little boy.

The problem was that instead of sitting Dan was running around in the tiny space holding musical instruments in his hand. One time he banged an instrument on the instructor's head. The other problem was that Liam wanted to do what Dan was doing, and so Daphne, his mom, hissed at me, "You better get a hold of Dan."

When it was free time for the kids Dan was delighted. He ran from one side of the room to the other. And then he started spinning. He spun and laughed and spun and laughed. 'He is having a blast,' I thought looking at him. But then I saw Alex looking at him from across the room. He was talking to another dad and then I saw his face freeze all of a sudden, focusing his gaze on Dan.

"I think there's something wrong," Alex said to me on the way home. "He did not participate like all the other kids."

We were walking the snowy New York City streets on our way home while Dan was sitting in his stroller.

"You are completely wrong!" I said. "There were parts that Dan did participate in, the less crowded ones. He played the piano with Liam. He was dancing around. It was not all bad."

But then pictures from the party flashed again in my mind.

"And he really wanted to come to the table for the cake part," I said. "There were just too many kids there already," I kept trying to convince him and also myself.

***

After the Diagnosis, when we would try to go places with Dan - and it could be a restaurant, store or museum – Dan would just do his own thing. At a restaurant he could wander to other tables and try to get food from strangers. There was a long time when he would run to random people and hug them. Or try and play with their toes, if they wore sandals or flip-flops. This bothered Alex tremendously.

My reaction to those incidents was different. I didn't worry about such behaviors that much. I just couldn't stand listening to Dan cry and whine. It drove me insane.

So while I would go crazy when he whined and I could not help him, Alex managed to stay calm and analyze the situation. He would accept that sometimes there was nothing we could do to help Dan and that we needed to wait it out. I, on the other hand, was tortured by the thought of not being able to help him.

Another difference between us was that while I was the strict one trying to do everything the therapists were telling us and watching Dan's strict diet, Alex wanted to have some fun. He would make up songs that Dan sang with him. This is how we discovered that Dan has an amazing memory. Alex sang long songs with him and had Dan fill in the blanks, and Dan always did. When they walked together it looked like they were having a conversation. Alex would sing, “When the devil went down to Georgia he was looking for a soul to...” and Dan would say, “Steal!” Alex would continue, “He was in a bind because he was way behind, so he was willing to make a...” and Dan would say, “Deal!” and so on. They would sing the whole song together.

This was an amazing thing that Alex could do. I was busy figuring out meaningful communication and I was not sure if this was even appropriate, but Dan loved it and this was something fun he did with his dad.

THE ENDING OF A FRIENDSHIP

February 2008

The breakup from my Israeli friend Dalia happened at the same time I was busy making all the changes in therapy for Dan.

Ever since we met, Dalia has made me question everything we were doing for Dan.

After she met Tova, Dalia commented, "She's way too soft, isn't she?"

When Dan started attending Happy Kids, she advised, "I wish you luck with this preschool, but honestly I don't think this will work. We failed completely in a similar setting for Nili in Israel."

Dalia criticized all the professionals we had been in contact with. Besides Dr. J. the pediatrician, who was their doctor too. We both had frequent visits to see him. Her baby boy kept on getting ear infections and I would take Gali in for the regular check ups. Dalia started comparing notes with me.

"Dr. J. told me last week that he thinks it's a miracle that Nili is still eligible for services. He can barely see traces of her special needs by now," Dalia said one day when I was at her house.

"Alex and I had such a nice visit with Dr. J. yesterday," I said on another day when Dalia came over with the kids. "He said it is possible that that even though Dan has difficulties now, most of them will go away eventually." I saw Dalia's face reddening.

It was the stupidest competition. Two grownup women sitting over coffee and comparing their special needs children through the eyes of their doctor.

After we saw the psychologist and I told Dalia her recommendations, she noted, "Isn't this therapy what they do for severe cases of autism?"

And then one day Dalia started complimenting Nili on how well she was treating Dan. At first I was not sure what she was talking about. I guessed it was one of those things that she did, since she was so obsessed with everything her daughter said.

In this case I was in for a surprise, because when I finally asked Dalia directly what she was saying, she said that Nili had been saying that she no longer wanted to play with Dan. "I think she sees a lot of her hardship in Dan. She sees her own difficulties magnified through him."

My heart sank. Until then I had felt like Dalia's house was a safe place for Dan in the sea of rejection we had been experiencing after the diagnosis. And to hear such a remark from a mother to a special needs child, for crying out loud!

From that day on I stopped seeing Nili as a beautiful girl with minor issues. All of her challenges started to bother me and I did not hide it from Dalia. Now not only was she criticizing me and mentioning stuff that was wrong with Dan, I was doing the same thing to her.

One day we came to their house and Nili insisted on coloring Gali's nails with a marker. I called Dalia to stop her.

When Dalia was bothered because she could not get Nili playdates with her friends from school, I was not as supportive as I could have been.

I did not like feeling like this, so I decided to take the initiative and talk to her about it. I wanted to straighten things out. I didn't want to compete with her about whose situation was worse. I didn't want to focus on the negative sides of our children. I wanted to go back to the way we were in the beginning: seeing the beauty in the kids and looking beyond the "problem."

I invited Dalia to go out for coffee. I felt like we would be more relaxed just the two of us.

"I am sorry I've been so impatient with Nili lately," I started.

Dalia nodded as if she had been expecting this apology.

"I understand. Your situation is different."

Different, she said, but she really meant "worse than mine."

"You see for a while I could not see what you were talking about, what was 'wrong' with her..." I stopped to take a breath and could hear an alarm going off in my head but could not stop. "I thought that everything was in the past and she already got over it. But now that you made me read everything, I do see, and it's hard. I wish she was over this already. I need to know that those things go away."

The moment these words slipped through my mouth I regretted it.

Dalia took a big breath and looked me in the eye in silence.

"You can only wish Dan was in Nili's situation. Any parent would wish that their special needs child could be in Nili's situation. You know that."

See? That denial! She does not even say the A word. Autism, I thought, your girl has autism.

But then again, was she not my mirror? And I was doing that too. When I would talk to people I would say, "He does not talk yet," or "He has a sensory integration problem," or even worse "He is really tired."

From that point on the conversation with Dalia just went downhill. It was obvious we would never meet or talk again.

I was alone. Again. And Dan was too. All of a sudden, the only place besides home that felt like home to him was gone. The only friend he had left was gone too.

Later on I learned that comparing children with special needs is not only mean, it's also pointless. I have seen many children who seemed very severe and then ended up doing very well, just as I have seen kids who seemed to be "slightly autistic" and then developed major challenges later on. Nobody knows how a child will end up. Each child has his own pace. The one thing a parent can do is find what moves the child and follow that. Find his or her sometimes-hidden gift. Everyone is good at something and happy doing it. The best is, to do everything you can at any given moment, and hope.

DAN'S NIGHT TERRORS

April 2008

That spring, when Dan was four, he started experiencing night terrors. His sleeping hasn't been easy since Gali was born, when he was three. Her loud crying would wake him up, but then the problem suddenly escalated and got out of control.

It started one night at 2 am. Dan woke, sat up abruptly, and hurried and got out of our bed. It seemed like he was running away from something. He ran through the corridor into the dark living room, screaming in fear. Alex and I tried to talk to him and hold him but he squirmed away and looked right through us.

This episode repeated every night for over a week. It lasted two to three hours each time, until Dan collapsed back to sleep, exhausted. He fell asleep again for the few hours left before morning came.

We were completely helpless. We knew about night terrors, where kids would behave like that. But we did not know how to solve it. One answer we kept on getting was that this is what happens sometimes with kids who have autism: Their sleep is disturbed and nobody knows why.

This answer was not good enough for me. Since I did not get a solution from the "regular" doctors, I decided to try my energy healers. I had a feeling that Maya would be the right person for the task.

***

December 2005

Maya was my friend Sharon's teacher. After watching my friend Sharon, who participated in Maya's workshops and classes, go through a positive personal growth, I decided to follow Sharon's advice and go meet with Maya myself. At that time Dan was almost two, we were in New York, and I was at a professional crossroad. I felt like Maya and her insights could help direct me.

I made a time to see Maya, trying to plan the time of the appointment so that Dan would be taking a nap when we got there. I wanted quiet time with her.

On the day of the appointment, Dan and I got in the car and soon after I started driving, he fell asleep. We arrived at Maya's building and I took Dan out of his car seat slowly and carefully. The plan was to place him in the stroller and let him sleep in it the whole appointment. Dan usually stayed asleep during such transitions. I pushed the stroller gently to the door to find out that Maya's clinic was on the third floor of a walk-up. I lifted the stroller and started climbing up the stairs. The bouncing and rocking woke Dan up and so I found myself at the door with a wide-awake, cranky, and jet-lagged two year old.

Maya greeted us at the door. She was a beautiful woman with short brown hair and big blue eyes. Everything about her said comfort and warmth. She looked like light was coming from within her.

She showed us into a room filled with large pillows. There were candles burning on the shelves along the walls. As soon as I walked in there I felt relaxed.

Maya sat down next to me on the pillows. She followed my gaze as I watched Dan running around, instead of taking his nap.

“It’s OK. He is safe here, don’t worry.”

I leaned back and looked at her.

She started: “Let’s see what you have told me,” she pulled out a piece of paper. She was referring to the “communication” she had already performed with my soul. “I asked you “how can I help you?” and you showed me a number of images. In many of your lives you were a really strong person, whether as a woman or a man. The first thing you showed me was of a man sitting at his desk with a gun. It was the time of the great depression in the United States and the man, you, was the owner of a big plant and was blaming himself for having to let his workers go. He was sitting there about to commit suicide. What are you blaming yourself for in this life, Shirley?” she asked, her voice soft.

I thought about what she had just asked me and could not come up with anything.

Maya continued: "You also showed me an image of yourself with your spiritual guide. You were locked in chains and you were asking for forgiveness. Apparently you have helped refugees in a big war. You were later captured and tortured for your actions. In the time after you died, you felt guilty for what you did. The similarity between these two lifetimes is that it was not your actions that were "wrong," it was the way your soul was strained because of the results. You know, Shirley, the soul needs nourishment too."

She took out a notebook and drew a well.

"If you use the water and use more and more, at some point you will get close to here," she drew a line close to the bottom, "and then you are left with just the mud. You need to make sure you don't get to the bottom. Find ways to fill the well."

I could certainly relate to what she drew. The times preceding our visit to Israel, were not easy. I lost my job and was home a lot with Dan. He was not an easy baby. In fact, he confused me. At times he was easy and followed a routine and at times it was hard to engage him or predict how he would react to certain places and activities.

The whole time Maya and I were talking, Dan was wandering around the room. Maya noticed that he was getting bored and gave him a paper and a box of pastels. Dan started drawing. When we were done Maya looked at what Dan drew and was amazed. He used every single crayon in the box and drew lines and lines on the paper. The result was a sea of different colors. "Look at how balanced he is," she said to me, "he used all the colors of all the different chakras." I looked at her with question and she explained: "Chakras are the centers of energy in our bodies. Each chakra is represents by a color. Dan used all of those colors. Here is the purple for the third eye and spirituality, the blue for communication, red for grounding, green for the heart… He is a very special boy, you know," she concluded.

***

When Dan was having the night terrors, I called Maya and explained to her what was going on. We had not been in touch since Dan was two and a half.

I told Maya what Dan was experiencing, about his language, about the unusual things happening. I told her that the doctors called Dan autistic and that I thought he was just seeing things differently.

Maya listened to me quietly. I could envision her nodding her head while I was talking. And then she said, "Shirley, you sound so different from the time we last met. You seem so much more aware. It sounds like you see things too!"

Then she promised to look into the night terrors. "Email me your full names and Dan's date of birth again, OK?"

Am I seriously doing this? I thought to myself, but I was desperate so I emailed her the information she needed. She called me back after a few days with a solution. First she told me about her communication with Dan: "At first he did not want to talk to me at all. He showed me the "souls of nature" that were surrounding him, in the form of butterflies and birds. You know, Shirley, because Dan is so sensitive, he has a hard time being "here" when there is negative energy around him. His way of coping with this hurtful energy is wandering to higher dimensions. When he hears Gali's voice, or any sound that startles him, it pulls him back to reality too fast, and he does not have a way of gathering himself back together. He is physically here, but he is still experiencing the other dimensions at the same time."

"What can I do?" I felt helpless.

"You can help him by guiding him back. I already talked to him about it and explained how I can help him when that happens. All you need to do is remind him what he and I talked about, OK?"

This all sounded very weird. But I felt like I had nothing to lose. My rule was just like the first time I went to see Teresa: Even if I do not get it, I will do it, as long as it helps.

The next night, like clockwork, at 2 a.m., Dan's night terrors began. He woke up screaming, pushed us away and ran in the dark apartment. I followed him and started saying what Maya told me to say. "Dan," I said softly, "Remember what Maya taught you? You can ask for help, just follow the light and the fairies..." Yes, that's what she said!

Within a few seconds Dan stopped screaming and started to listen to my voice. After only one hour, with much less screaming, Dan was sound asleep. I was relieved, but I did not completely believe it yet. Yes, it was one hour instead of three but it could still be a coincidence.

The next night, at 2 a.m., Dan woke up again. I did the exact same thing, following Maya's instructions. This time it took only 10 minutes.

The night after that Dan did not wake up at all.

I did it! Maya taught me and I did it. I was so happy and proud. And I also realized this was not all for nothing. What my healers have been telling me all this time was true. There was an alternative way to help Dan, with these healing tools. I followed my intuition, and I managed to help him.

INTERNAL BATTLE: NATURAL HEALING V. MODERN MEDICINE

May 2008

After reading literature about the connection between vaccines and autism, I became very angry with medical doctors everywhere. How could they continue to vaccinate infants when it was damaging them? I stopped trusting modern medicine and put my faith in alternative treatments.

It was an incident with Gali that made me rethink.

When Gali was born the pediatrician told me that until she was two or three years old we wouldn't know for sure if she had autism. Even though I didn't feel like she had it, she managed to scare me a few times, when she got sick. When she got common colds and ear infections, and stopped being her alert and happy self, I would worry.

When she was 13 months old the pediatrician noticed that she had fluid in her ears that would not clear. At that time she began responding less to our calling her name. I did not put the two together. I was only scared of autism. I was hoping the fluid would clear on its own, because the other option was to put tubes in her ears. I was really scared of that because the procedure required general anesthesia.

I tried to heal her naturally. The naturopathic doctor I was seeing for Dan at the time suggested that Gali drink goat milk instead of cow's milk. She believed that cow's milk created nasal congestion. I had heard that before so I followed her advice. Gali got the worst stomachache so I immediately stopped.

At the visit to the ear, nose and throat doctor I begged him to give me one more month before scheduling the surgery. "I know this sounds crazy, but I have heard of situations where the fluids go away," I told him. I was referring to my new age and healing books, of course. And to my energy healing web sites.

That night I had a dream. I saw Jesse, Gali's teacher. She was sobbing. She could not talk because she was so distraught. "What happened?" I asked her. I had never seen her this way. She could not talk back but I saw her looking at Gali. "What's wrong?" I asked. "Please tell me!" But she would not say a thing. She just kept looking into my eyes and crying. I woke up terrified. What if in real life there was something wrong with Gali?

When the month was over we took Gali to the hospital to get the tubes procedure done. I was worried enough to go with it. Alex was relieved. He would have done it long before, but he wanted me to be at peace.

The day after the procedure Gali went back to school.

"Watch her carefully and let us know if anything is different," I asked of Jesse when I hugged Gali goodbye.

When I came to pick her up that day I saw her running around with her friends while the teachers were watching them, smiling.

"Gali!" I called her name.

She turned back as soon as she heard my voice and ran towards me. I picked her up and lifted her in the air and then held her tight, tears of relief running down my cheeks.

“Oh, she is back!” Jesse smiled at me.

In the following days Gali started talking so much I could not believe it. Is this how babies are? They develop so fast?

It made me think. Ever since autism came into my life and I could not get answers from doctors about it, I stopped believing in “regular” medicine. I thought I would find the solutions in natural healing, just as I did for my migraines in the past. I was angry with the pediatrician and other doctors for labeling Dan and not understanding him. But now that regular medicine helped Gali, I decided to be more open to doctors in the future.

THE WORLD OF SPECIAL EDUCATION

August 2008

In the beginning, Alex and I decided to give Dan any and every therapy we could so he would get better soon. At first, it was just a few half hours of speech therapy a week. Then we added occupational therapy. Then we started giving Dan many more hours of speech therapy. When Dan first started going to Happy Kids we provided an hour a day of speech therapy for him. Twenty hours a month.

And when things stopped working we added more therapy on top of that. We followed the advice of the psychologist who told us that Dan needed behavioral therapy, and we tried to add that to the time Dan had after he got home from Happy Kids and on weekends. We still believed that if we did everything right, Dan would be autism-free one day soon.

Juggling all these new therapies and a baby was a lot. Wednesdays were the worst. On

Wednesdays Dan had occupational therapy at 5:30 pm. I would pick the kids up from Happy Kids, bring them home, and then leave Gali with a babysitter to take Dan to see Sydney. Then, when we got back home, I would let Dan do whatever he wanted and I would grab Gali for a big hug. Then I would give her a bath and put her to bed.

One Wednesday we got stuck in traffic on our way home. "Please please be awake when I get there," I prayed while picturing Gali's face. Dan was whining in the back of the car. He was tired and hungry. I knew how he felt. I felt the exact same way. Only *I* had to keep it together for a little longer. We finally got through all the lights and into the parking lot. Dan was exhausted. He couldn't move. I decided I didn't have time for convincing. I hung my purse on my shoulder and picked him up. I had the keys in my pocket to open the building door but then I saw someone opening it. If I made it there in time I wouldn't have to put Dan down to use the key. Just a few more steps. I was running, with Dan in my arms and all the snacks and Dan's special sippy cup threatening to fall out of my bag. My shoe fell off and I had to stop. I bent down to fix it and then my purse fell, and everything rolled onto the ground. The door slammed.

"Please be up," I kept on praying.

We made it to the elevator. The elevator beeped, counting the floors.

I opened the door, dropped my bags in the doorway and rushed into the living room, where I pictured Gali playing with the babysitter.

She was sitting there by herself. The babysitter.

"Oh, she fell asleep 30 minutes ago," she said when she saw the question in my eyes, "She was completely exhausted."

When Alex came home that night he found me sobbing in my bathrobe. I had just come out from sobbing in the shower and was too tired to even put my pajamas on. "I did not get to be with her all day...."

This one moment was enough.

He understood.

Alex finally exploded that Saturday morning.

That morning, the plan was for me and Gali to take a stroll downtown while Dan was getting his behavioral therapy.

Our newly appointed behavior therapist was late and then finally appeared at the door with her two little daughters. Alex and I stood there in shock to hear “This one is sick so she did not want to stay with the babysitter. And then this one did not want to stay either.” Of course it made complete sense to her to bring them to our house and let them play with Gali’s baby toys while she was working with Dan. But then her daughters needed her all the time she was there. We finally sent her on her way when she said, “See, I do not think the schedule is working.”

You see, everyone always stresses how important it is to get treatment early and yet it is so hard to find good treatment and the right therapist for the kids. So many parents are trapped, struggling to find out which therapy and/or therapist is right or not being able to pay for the person they do find.

After this incident Alex said to me, “We cannot depend on individual people like that. This one comes late, this one’s child is sick so she is bringing her with her, and it is all way too expensive right now.”

I could not believe he said that.

"Too expensive for Dan? We are saving his life!" I screamed in tears.

"But what we are doing is not working. I can't let you run the show anymore. This is too much."

I sat there sobbing.

"What about that school you told me about? Good School?" he said in a calmer voice.

Good School was a private special education school that I went to see when we first were looking. At that time, we thought it was too much for Dan because the kids who went there were more challenged than he was.

"Well," Alex said, "Dan has not 'come out of his bubble' yet. What we're doing doesn't get him where we want. And what we are spending per year is almost twice the tuition for Good School. I want to go see it myself."

I was having a hard time with this. I did not want to let go of the typical world so easily. I was not ready. 'Just not special education,' I thought.

They loved him so much at Happy Kids and they believed in him. That helped me keep believing too. I wanted so much to show Dan that I thought he belonged here, in the typical world.

Parents link children to the world. When babies are born we hold them, feed them and nurture them. When they grow we are their source of information, we are the source of self-confidence. We help create them and who they are. A parent can turn a child into someone beautiful and confident and great, or can make the same child miserable and fearful. It is like programming a computer. What you program, is what you will get.

I wanted to teach Dan that he could do anything.

Alex thought he needed to get more tools before he could do that.

So I agreed to go see Good School again.

When Alex and I went to see Good School we met with Myra, the director.

Myra was a woman in her fifties. The best way to describe her is as Albert Einstein's female twin. She had an appearance that made me think of Einstein, and she had that brilliance in her eyes.

We could immediately tell that she was really good at what she does. Two seconds from the time we entered the room with Dan, she was chasing him, playing with him and making him talk.

She ignored Alex and me completely and focused only on Dan. And he was so happy to be there.

You see, children with autism usually dread new places. Their senses are so heightened that going into a new place usually means they will have to get used to many new things. Their brains have to put so much effort into filtering the new information. They can become very uncomfortable and so they try to avoid new places. That's how Dan usually was.

But that day at Good School with Myra he behaved as if he had known her forever. He played and had a great time. Alex and I sat quietly and watched. We were scared to say anything that might ruin the beautiful sight we were witnessing.

At one point Myra took a quick break from playing with Dan and looked at us.

"You know, back in the day they would never call what your son has 'autism.' Look at him, he is so social."

Alex and I looked at each other and then at her. I could see the hope in Alex's eyes and I knew I must have looked exactly the same. Myra awakened something in both of us.

"I think Dan might have something called Apraxia. It's a disorder that interferes with a person's ability to speak. I have experts for that here at the school."

Alex and I remained quiet but our faces must have shown the way we were feeling so she went on.

"I think Dan should spend one year maximum here. And then I would like to see him go straight to first grade. I think he is really smart and he will do great academically."

Alex and I looked at each other. Our hearts were about to explode. Mainstream? First grade? This lady just offered us the moon.

On our way to the car Alex did not need to say 'I told you so.' I did it for him. "I can't believe we did not come here sooner," I said. "Think of how our lives would have been different. All of us."

We both felt like we were on a cloud. You see, parents of children with autism are constantly under constrains of stress and fear. Even when we are happy there is always that feeling of 'what will happen? How will she/he end up?' We learn to live with it because you cannot obsess about it all the time. It is those rare moments of hope and relief that make us aware of it. When someone comes to us with good news and we feel like life may be good after all, the heavy veil is lifted and we feel like normal people. This usually lasts just a short while, but it is so worth it.

THE ALLERGIST

November 2008

After we could no longer keep the diet the way the naturopathic doctor suggested, Alex and I decided to take Dan to see Dr. B., an allergist and nutritionist.

The fact that Dr. B was an M.D. made Alex get on board with my new path. You see Alex is a professor. As part of his work he does research. He specializes in probability. He knows how to analyze statistics. When I was exploring treatments for Dan he always wanted to know what kind of research had been done to prove the effectiveness of the treatment and the credentials of the person who was offering the treatment. He was very against alternative treatments that had no scientific evidence base.

Dr. B. was very well known and respected throughout the country. He had the nurse draw blood from our poor screaming Dan, and sent it to the lab with a long form to test for all different kinds of allergies. When the test results came back, it turned out that Dan had an allergy to sugar. That explained why he was so miserable eating all the gluten-free but sugar-filled foods that we had given him in the previous months. Apparently when we were doing that he developed yeast overgrowth in his gut. The doctor said he might have had it before, due to the illness he had at age two, but being on a diet that was high in sugar and fruit made it much worse. I later learned that yeast in the gut could often cause the symptoms of autism, like stimming and repetitive behaviors, and how it might cause pain leading to "unexplained" tantrums.

Dr. B had a plan for us: "Give him this," he said handing me a tiny bottle. It was a special allergy treatment. "No sugar," he continued. "That's what feeds the yeast and also creates those ups and downs in the brain. Fewer carbs, because they break down to sugar quickly," he went on. "I want most of his intake to be protein. That's what our bodies are made of and that's what he should eat. And a spoon of fish oil once a day. Don't put it in anything like juice. Just give it to him. He needs to know it is good for him. He will take it."

'Sure he will,' I thought as I sat there, completely shocked by this line of instructions, with no clue how to implement them into Dan's life.

"Oh, and he can eat gluten. I don't see a problem there," said Dr. B., still looking at his chart, finally giving me one less thing to worry about.

What a complete shift. I was happy about being able to give Dan bread. And as soon as we started giving him bread again, Dan got better. He stopped behaving like a war survivor and his tantrums stopped.

The fish oil part was just messy. Dan would not take it on a spoon, of course, so I mixed it up with juice in his sippy cup. You should have smelled my dishwasher after I put that cup in there by mistake!

Amazingly enough, Dan did learn to take the fish oil with a spoon. He also responded well to the natural allergy drops the doctor gave me in that little bottle. Dan's digestive system healed shortly after we started following this Doctor's instructions. His stools became normal again.

I was so happy that I kept on increasing the protein and reducing the sugar. Eventually Dan started eating oven-roasted salmon, healthy beef frankfurters, beef from the stew, and vegetables.

It was not easy to get him to do that. At first he wouldn't even touch those foods. It was the doctor who helped me.

"What kind of texture does he like?" he asked me on one of my visits.

Dan liked crunchy things. So I sliced the healthy beef frankfurters and baked them in the oven, making them into beef chips. Dan loved them. I had to do that only once or twice more and after that Dan would eat them cooked because he got used to the taste and liked it.

I came up with creative solutions to replace the sweets Dan craved. I made ice cream with Stevia, a natural sweetener. It was the only sweetener Dr. B would let me use because it did not raise the blood sugar level. I baked brownies with a special kind of xylitol.

Dan did really well.

It was not easy for Alex and me, however. We had to give up so many foods that we liked because if we hid them in the house, Dan could find them. Dan was allowed only one serving a day and if he saw fruit, he wanted all of it. Luckily, he was at Good School by this time, and they only served kids what their parents sent from home. While Gali still got her fruit at day care, and I was comfortable that I was not depriving her of valuable nutrients, Alex and I were desperately craving fruit.

Once I went grocery shopping in the evening and got a bag of cherries. We sat together on the sofa and finished the whole bag, so Dan wouldn't find it in the morning. That evening life *was* a bowl of cherries for us.

The low-sugar/high-protein diet improved our lives so much that we kept following it strictly. Dan was much calmer. His stools became normal. He was doing well at school.

But there was another price of not giving Dan sugar. It meant we could not eat out at all with the kids. We could barely *be* out with Dan anywhere if there was a chance that he would see the forbidden foods. One day we needed to get something at the mall and Dan spotted the candy store. I was inside a store with Gali, and

Alex chased Dan, who bolted out of the play area and ran to the candy store. When Gali and I joined Alex and Dan, I saw Dan with one lollipop in his mouth and two more in his hand.

"Look how happy he is," Alex said tearfully. I was heartbroken. He *was* happy, of course, but it was not doing him any good. Yet part of me felt just like Alex: Let's let this little person be a kid!

One day on our way home from our favorite park, we stopped at a Starbucks so I could get coffee. Alex waited in the car with the kids. Dan saw me going into the store and associated the Starbucks logo with the amazing marble cakes we used to buy there for him, in the days before the diet. (See, kids with autism can recognize brands!) When I came out without his cake, Dan started to cry and would not stop the whole way home. Alex and I did not understand why he was so upset. At that point we still didn't realize how much he knew, this little guy.

It is so easy to assume that if your child does not talk they do not understand the world around them. The more I meet kids with autism, the more I see the truth is the exact opposite. The kids are so aware, but they do not have a way of showing it.

They can't talk so they can't tell us, but they experience the exact same feelings we do. Imagine how you would feel if you had to go through life, unable to share your feelings with anyone. Frustrating, right? Yet that's how our little ones feel most of the time. They learn to cope for the most part, but sometimes they just can't take it anymore.

That's what happened to Dan that day in the car when I got coffee at Starbucks but did not get him cake. And it must have happened hundreds of times but we just did not get it. His mind created the thought "I want that cake they used to get me in a place just like this. When Mom would get that exact same drink she would also get a brown bag with a cake in it. Why did she forget to give it to me today?"

THE AUTISM MOMS

January 2009

I met them at a birthday party organized by a smart autism mom from Good School. This mom simply sent invitations to school and asked the teacher to give them to all the kids in her child's age group. Being new to this school, I did not know anyone yet. I spotted the opportunity and brought Dan to the party.

We arrived at a spacious indoor playground filled with climbers, slides and swings. Dan ran to the ball pit and began chewing on the balls. I looked around. The other kids were each playing in their own corner. I glanced at the other parents, standing peacefully and watching the kids and realized that here, it was OK. The kids were having fun, and that was all that mattered.

The real party was for us, the moms. We inhaled each other. Just like me, the other autism moms did not get to socialize. Like Dan, their kids did not have play-dates. They did not go to the regular classes other kids went to, like music or gymnastics. They never played independently in the playground in a way that enabled their moms to talk to other parents.

Just like me, at a certain point in their lives, the autism moms found themselves separated from the "normal" world. For most it was around the time of the diagnosis or when things in their child's life started to "go wrong."

Therefore just like me, all the moms were lonely. That's why this party was nothing less than air for us.

And you had the full selection of moms to choose from.

There was the stressed out mom. This mom never leaves a rock unturned. She knows all the autism therapies available. She is always looking to learn more. At this point she has earned her theoretical Ph.D. in autism and its treatment. She quit her job and was dedicating her life to healing her child.

This mom's child was naturally on *the diet*, which meant that all the food he ate was gluten free, casein free, sugar free, you-name-it free. Everything had to be organic and he was getting a number of supplements that put my grandmother's selection of pills to shame. He was also going through a special cleansing procedure in order to "clean his body from all the shit."

The stressed out mom believed that her son's autism originated from the vaccines he was given as a baby, and she was doing everything possible to undo the damage caused to his body.

The next mom was the mom in denial. Her child went to the autism school together with the other kids at this party, but she believed it was just "for now," because the whole thing was an innocent mistake. Her child will soon be better and out of there. This mom looked with pity at the other kids and the other moms, who were *really* in this, thinking "poor them."

Then there was the depressed mom. She just went through another round of evaluations by a child psychologist and received yet another assurance of her child's diagnosis of "severely autistic." As always she went in hoping to hear something new, something encouraging. She thought her child was in a much better place this time. The expert thought differently and that is what counts. The depressed mom was taking time to process the news and in the meantime just could not see the point of this miserable life.

That's the thing about autism. The numerous ways it presents itself and the different ways that children progress through it are very confusing. Nobody knows how any child will end up, especially when they are young. So when you come to an evaluation you always have your hopes up. "Maybe this person will finally tell me that at some point things will be different." And yet again you get depressed, just like at the time of the first diagnosis at age two or three.

On the other end of the spectrum, you had the mom whose child was about to be mainstreamed. Oh, that is exactly where you want to be if your child has autism. You have been through it, served your time, and now you are released. You and your child will belong to the typical world from now on. The smile on this mom's face could not have been bigger. Everyone loved her and everyone wanted to be her, including me.

If I am to be perfectly honest, I have been and still am, each and every one of these moms.

At the party, when I looked around at the other moms, I felt safe. For the first time in a while, I felt like I belonged.

When the kids were having cake I asked them, "does anyone want to meet for lunch or something next week?"

My heart was pounding. What if they all ignore me? What if I was imagining the feeling of "we are in this together?"

Depressed mom was the first one who stopped cleaning her daughter's hand with an antibacterial wipe and lifted her eyes: "I'd love to!" she almost yelled.

"I'm around," said stressed-out-mom.

"Me too," said mom-in-denial.

I could not believe it but we all agreed on a day for the coming week.

At that moment, I knew there was hope. I was not the only one lonely and longing for friendship.

What I did not know yet, was that these women were going to be not only my friends but also my sisters. They were to become the rocks I could lean on and the islands I could swim to.

On the day I went to lunch with my new autism-mom-friends, I started to see my life in a different light. There was something right about being with people who shared your situation. It was not the commiserating part of it, because we did not engage with that. It was the relief of knowing, that the person listening to you is going through the same things you are on a daily basis, and feeling the same way you are feeling: scared, angry and insecure.

Each one of our kids had a different story, but we all had something in common: Our tough and endless quest to find a solution, a cure. There were so many treatments to choose from. There was not enough money or time to try them all. We all knew that the clock was ticking, and we had to treat the kids when they're young.

I enjoyed being surrounded by all these strong women, and to learn how similar our paths are.

That just like me they lost many friends after the diagnosis.

That just like me their lives were completely out of balance.

That just like me they couldn't work.

That just like me they were arguing with their husbands.

And that just like me they tried any and every treatment known to man.

They were my new "mirrors" and this time I liked my reflection a lot. Yes, we were focused on our children, but we attempted to keep that focus calm and sane.

The first lunch turned into more lunches, and then dinners and drinks. We came to rely on each other for advice. We exchanged information about doctors, therapists, teachers, diets, and any aspect of our complex worlds.

That first birthday party turned into many more parties. Finally our children were invited to birthday parties and they had friends to invite to their own. We – and they - were no longer alone.

MY AUTISTIC HEALER

February 2009

I first read about Joseph in one of my Israeli healing books. The story described Joseph as being severely autistic until he was eleven years old. He had all the typical symptoms and behaviors associated with autism and he was non-verbal. The doctors did not give his parents much hope.

When Joseph turned 11, a mysterious miracle occurred and he began to speak fluently. Doctors and specialists examined him in an attempt to understand what had happened, yet to this day, nobody could provide an explanation.

His parents told him that at first, he told them that all that time he had been surrounded by colorful clouds and rainbows; that angels and spirits and beautiful beings were flying around him; and he saw beautiful temples. He told them that where he had been beings communicated without talking. The language was one of colors and feelings. Nothing he said made sense to them, but shortly after he began talking, he ceased telling those tales and focused on learning about the world around him, until he became part of it.

As soon as I read Joseph's story I knew I had to contact him.

I dialed the number from the book. When Joseph picked up I told him I needed help.

"It's for your son, right?"

"Yes, he is 5. His name is..."

"Don't tell me. It has a D in it."

"Dan."

"Yes. You live far away from your family, but there is a family member whom Dan loves very much, and who lives within driving distance of you. He works with computers."

"Benny," I said slowly. My uncle lived near Boston.

I was impressed with the way Joseph knew these things, yet that was not why I called him, so I did not encourage him to tell me more. He must have sensed that, because he quickly asked: "So how can I help you?"

"I want you to teach me how to communicate with Dan."

I also wanted to know more about what happened to him before he turned 11.

"When I "came back," I did not recognize my parents. The only memory I had of them was from age two. I remember everything in detail: how my parents and I were sitting in the kitchen and my dad was feeding me. The food was too spicy for me. I left my body and I was floating up by the ceiling looking at everything from above. And then I saw black shadows moving around me. They took me with them and put me in a white room. The light was so bright that it hurt. I was there for a long time. I could not tell how long. Time did not matter there. It was all the same. One day, a very old soul came to me and told me: "Your mother is praying for you. Do you want to come?" And I came," he said laughing. "And that's when they tell me I came back."

His story seemed completely insane however when I spoke with him he sounded normal. I could not fully believe he was as severely autistic as he described, yet I had a feeling he could help me understand Dan and his world.

"I believe that parents are the healers of their children," he said to me. "Autism is not what they think it is: It's not an illness, it's a language. I can teach you the special language that Dan communicates in."

I was silent for a moment, thinking how up to that point, I had been told that autism is not curable; I did not think Dan was communicating; and I did not know what more I could do for him, besides looking for the best doctors and experts that would hopefully cure him.

To help me grasp his ideas, Joseph gave me a visual description: "Imagine that you are Dan's channel to the world; you can help him connect with people here. You need to clean that channel from negative energy and enable Dan to use it."

Since Joseph was in Israel and I was in Connecticut, we agreed on a weekly therapy session over the phone.

When we began our first therapy session, Joseph told me I had to "stop the big movement." I had no idea what he meant, so he explained that kids like Dan could feel things that we go through. When I was having emotional highs and lows, Dan could feel that, "and it hurts."

I was in complete shock: How did Joseph know? Different people must experience the difficult task of parenting a child with autism in different ways. Some moms are in denial. Some are depressed. How did he know after five minutes of talking to me that I was on an emotional rollercoaster? It was true: one day I could believe that Dan would be OK, and then the next day I would feel completely hopeless.

Joseph went on to explain what Dan must be seeing and hearing: "He is exposed to information you are not even aware of, like the bright lights for example. Sometimes they just appear and it hurts."

When I told him how Dan could not stand the loud buses at the school parking lot, he said: "I know. Those beasts are so noisy." He had a weird way of talking sometimes but it helped me understand. I felt like I had discovered an open window into Dan's head. I wanted to learn everything I could about his mind: the autistic mind.

Joseph concluded our first call with three assignments: make an effort to stop the emotional rollercoaster; watch the stars and tell him what I saw and how I felt, and watch the movie “The Matrix.”

“Why?”

“Watch it and *you* will tell me.”

The last assignment was the easiest of the three. I went online and ordered the DVD of the movie “The Matrix.” Joseph mentioned another movie that we would get to later, “What the bleep do we know,” so I decided to order that one too. Because the online orders usually came in three I added one more film for fun. After all, the first two were ‘work.’

Star watching was more complicated. Joseph mentioned “the bright lights,” that he could still see, and that he was certain Dan could see them as well. I wondered if that was what he wanted me to experience. It was impossible to see the stars properly from our apartment window. We lived downtown and other buildings surrounded ours. I figured I had to leave the apartment at nighttime and find a place where I could watch the stars.

I volunteered to go to the grocery store one night. Before I got into the car I looked at the stars. When I looked at them, some of them really sparkled. I thought these were probably the bright lights Joseph mentioned. I believed I had completed this assignment successfully.

Apparently not. When I spoke to Joseph the next time, it turned out this was *not* the purpose of the assignment. I had to try again. “Go to a planetarium,” he suggested. “Write down your thoughts as soon as the show ends.”

So I did. I went all the way to New York City to meet my friend Lea and we went to the Museum of Natural History. How sweet of Lea to join me on this unusual task. She placed her little baby in a sling, and we tried to find a seat in the showroom, moving through the deep blackness. There were hundreds of school students there on a field trip. We heard the teachers hushing the kids. “Shhhh” Lea hushed her baby, smiling at me in the dark.

The show started and I let myself sink into the sights. The solar system performed a dance of light before our eyes as the narrator was explaining the history of our little planet and the objects surrounding it in space. When the lights were turned back on, I got it: I felt the endlessness of space; I sensed the history and the infinite time our universe existed; I realized how big it was; I grasped the endless wisdom that created it.

The feeling I had in my body was new: a combination of lightness, almost dizzy, in the body and at the same time clarity in the mind and serenity. I knew I had felt like this once before. A memory from when I was a little girl came to me. I was in my bed when my hands started to feel a bit numb. It was not exactly numbness. It was more like a slight feeling of electricity going through them. And then I pictured our world and I wondered what happens when our world ends. What was there beyond it? And I saw that beyond was another world. And then another. As if all the universes were connected in a huge quilt. One ends and then starts another, for eternity.

When I talked to Joseph later that week and told him my thoughts after the planetarium show, he said I got the assignment right.

APPRECIATE YOURSELF

February 2009

During our next conversation, Joseph surprised me: He told me to appreciate myself. "You are doing so much for Dan. You are doing so much for everyone. I want you to appreciate this, appreciate yourself. Because you are a wonderful person and a great mom."

When I met my autism-mom-friend Michelle later that week, I told her what Joseph said to me. I was going to joke about it, when I saw the look in her eyes: deep compassion. Before I could decide whether to cry or laugh hysterically with embarrassment, she stepped forward and hugged me really tight. "He is right, you know?" she whispered, "You are amazing. Everyone sees that."

That hug convinced me that Joseph had a point: I needed to appreciate myself more. Deep down I knew the reason I had not done that: Because if I took the time to get in touch with myself, to get that appreciation, I would fall apart. I put so much effort into maintaining the shield. At first it was the shield against the world, the so-called denial. Now it was the shield "against" myself, or the woman that I used to be: The woman who had a happy life and wanted children and love. But then at some point life took all of her dreams away. It was time for me to look this woman in the eye: acknowledge all of what I wanted and was not getting; recognize all the sorrow I felt and all of the fear; admit that life did not turn out the way I wanted at all.

Joseph gave me a new assignment: to drive around with Dan in the car. Dan loved to be in the car and we were driving for 25 minutes each way to school, so that one was easy. Soon after Joseph defined driving with Dan as an assignment, I noticed how my mind was at ease while we were riding in the car. I began getting thoughts and ideas and was having conversations in my head with different people: Especially with my mother and with Dr. J., Dan's pediatrician.

In both conversations, I would imagine telling them that Dan was OK. It was a happy story in my mind where Dan suddenly began to talk. In my vision, I pictured myself calling my parents and when my dad picked up the phone asking him to put my mom on the line as well. "Mom, Dad," I would say, "Dan is OK. He started talking last night. It is all done." There would be silence on the line and then I would hear my mom sobbing and my dad trying to catch his breath. In the other vision I had, Dan and I were going to a check up with Dr. J., and the doctor was completely stunned when he saw Dan. "I cannot believe this miracle," he would say. And I would reply: "I told you so!"

When I told Joseph about those visions I was having, he said: "Shirley, this is doubt."

As soon as he said that, warm tears started running down my cheeks. Something unlocked in me. I understood what he meant. *I* was the one needing convincing, not the doctor. *I* was the one who would be surprised if Dan magically healed, not my mother. The conversations were actually with myself, working hard on believing. Trying to make peace between the "me" who was blindly believing that Dan would be OK, and the "me" who needed more persuasion. Like there were two forces living within me side by side: the "mainstream" that labeled Dan as autistic, and that characterized me as being in denial; and the spiritual that believed Dan is beautifully different, and that there is hope.

***

I have to admit that the assignment of appreciating myself is an ongoing one. I need to remind myself every day all day what an important and meaningful task I am performing, by raising Dan and taking care of our family. Sometimes, especially when things get tough, and they still do, it is hard not to miss the life I had before autism.

Just a few months before this book came out, I got a surprising message from someone who belongs my former life. I was contacted by one of my soldiers on Facebook. I was surprised that he wanted to get in touch with me. I always believed my soldiers – all men – did not like me at all. I was very tough on them.

***

After graduating high school I was drafted into the Israeli Defense Force, just like every 18 year old in Israel. I was stationed with the Air Force and was accepted – after challenging tests - to the Officers' Course. I specialized in communications, a male-dominated field. As a young Second Lieutenant I was stationed in one of the most fascinating Wings and was very lucky to be involved in complex operations involving development and testing of state of the art missiles and the launching of satellites into space. I had to hit the ground running and learn everything about the special communications systems and equipment involved because as soon as I was stationed, we had to provide communication for a very big operation.

I remember when my commander took me to see the missile the day before the big launch. We drove along the sparkling blue waters of the Mediterranean Sea. Light brown clean sand stretched on both sides of the road. We arrived at the huge gray building, a location only few people could know. He took me through the winding corridors to a large room with a glass wall looking at the missile. We had to wear special white overalls on top of our beige Air Force uniform and special pads to cover our shoes. This was so we wouldn't bring even a spec of dust into the lab where the missile was. When we were ready he opened the door and we went in. The missile was standing in the middle, upright. Huge. Majestic. It was as though by entering the lab we were transported into a different world. We felt so small compared to the missile, and very proud of being chosen to be involved in something so big, so important.

The next day in the operations room – which looked so similar to the operations rooms you see in the movies, that I get feelings of longing when I go see a military or space film – there were no words to describe the excitement. Hundreds of officers and engineers were present, every person aware of their part in this unbelievably important operation. They used to call me "Air" because of the saying we used to have in the Air Force that "Communications is like air and water. When you have it, you don't notice it, yet you can absolutely not do without it."

We arrived there at dawn to make sure that everything was working properly. The huge operations room was still empty. Slowly people started to arrive, manning their positions and checking that everything was in place. As we got closer to the actual launch you could feel the tension in the air. All the parties involved had been working on this operation for months. "Test run," the head commander announced. He was a little man with short, spiked red hair. And then he started to countdown. "Ten, nine, eight, seven, six, five, four, three, two, one, top!"

I couldn't wait for the actual launch. The levels of adrenalin in the room had rocketed by now. We had to go through a few more tests, and then it was time. "Positions," announced the redhead. The silence in the room was so absolute. You could only hear the beeping from the machines. "Real run," he said and my heart was about to explode with nervousness and excitement. “Ten, nine, eight, seven, six, five, four, three, two, one, top!” And by a push of a button he did it. He launched the missile.

There was a study that compared the stress levels of autism moms and soldiers in combat. I have not been in combat so I cannot testify to that. I have only been in complex operations such as the one I just recounted. We were very nervous and very stressed and so many things could have gone wrong and put people in danger. So I can tell you this. When I get through an episode with Dan where he has self- injurious and aggressive behaviors, when I manage to find the strength to help him through it, I feel just like after that launch: proud and strong, like I’ve done the most important thing in the world.

***

‘How are you doing? I see you have two kids,’ wrote my soldier when he found me on Facebook. ‘I’m OK, had a somewhat rough morning, sorry if I sound whiny, it’s hard raising a child with autism,’ I wrote back. ‘Do not call my badass officer whiny!’ he wrote, shattering my shield and bringing me to tears. See to him I was badass, and I had no idea. I thought they hated my guts for being tough and making them work hard. I realized the true reason I was crying was because I used to be that. A badass officer. A woman making it in a man's world, where no woman has gone before her. Now dealing with autism I did not feel like a success at all.

When my stepson came to visit us from college I told him about the message I got and he started to laugh. I waved the wooden spoon I was holding – I was cooking pasta - to pretend to hit him. "No," he said, "You're not getting it. It must have been so much easier to be a Communications Officer in the Air Force than to be the autism mom that you are now. I put my spoon down in silence. He was absolutely right.

Blog Post from my website May 19, 2011

I've Been to "Italy"

Remember the beautiful story about how when you are expecting a baby it is like planning a trip to Italy and when you have a child with autism it is like you end up in Holland?

So I live in "Holland." Even though I get to speak some "Italian" with my typical girl, my life still happens in Holland. I know everything there is to know about special education; special diets; and treatments for autism. You name it.

But this week I visited a friend in New York and spent some time just by myself with her family. It was like a trip to "Italy."

She is a very good friend and had always been a model mom to me. She is raising 4 kids in New York City and enjoys every minute of it. When I lived there I was stressed out a lot. (Maybe because I did not know yet what was different about my child. It was only after we left that we got the diagnosis.)

But back to Italy.

In Italy nobody wakes up at 3 am for the day. You actually need to wake the kids up for school.

In Italy the kids get themselves ready for school. You don't even need to tell them. They get dressed by themselves.

In Italy you can make the same lunch for all 4 kids. There are no special diets or special requests.

In Italy the kids walk to school by themselves at ages 9 and 7. The younger ones go with you and listen to you and follow directions at all time.

It is so much easier in Italy!!

But yet I missed Holland.

And when I came back home I got the biggest hug from Dan. No words. Just a hug.

And I knew that I would not ever want to switch.

Thank you my friend for the most wonderful 24 hours of culture and fun.

And for the perspective.

TOILET TRAINING

March 2009

Toilet training can be such an ordeal when a child has autism. Every child has to go through it, and yet some have it easier than others. Children with autism are guaranteed to have it hard.

Alex and I were dreading toilet training Dan so much that we did not really try seriously until Dan was five years old. We had made half-hearted attempts before that, but nothing worked. I believe it was my process with Joseph that awakened the empowered and enabled me to handle the different challenges in Dan's and my life, including toilet training.

When Dan started attending Good School, they started him very early on a gadget called "Tinkle Tunes." It was a simple little device they put in his diaper, and it made a sound once it got wet. As soon as it would start playing the music, the teachers would rush Dan to the toilet.

After a few weeks of using it successfully at school, it was time for Alex and I to try it at home. Nancy, the teacher in charge of toilet training at the school, instructed us carefully about what we were supposed to do. She told me how to activate the device and how to use it in Dan's diaper. She told me to tape a chart to the bathroom door, so we could track the times we were taking Dan to the toilet to pee. After a few days we would be able to predict when he is going and take him before he even starts to go in his diaper.

When I told my friend Sally about the plan, she suggested that I try putting Dan in underwear when we were home.

"Dan needs to understand why he needs to go to the toilet instead of peeing in his diaper. After all, he's been using the diaper his whole life. Put him in underwear and explain that big boys wear underwear, and he has to go to the toilet, because if he pees in his underwear it will get wet."

I did exactly as she said. To my surprise, Dan was toilet trained for peeing in just a few days. I couldn't believe it. I always hated parents who told stories like this, about children miraculously getting toilet trained. I never believed them.

Now I do. Sometimes children surprise us, even children who have autism.

So toilet training for peeing – check.

But then we had to move on to "number two." And that was some number. Dan understood pretty quickly that he was not supposed to do his business in the diaper, but he had a much harder time accepting that he should do it in the toilet. Instead, he held it in for hours, just so he would not have to go to the toilet. When he had to go, he would get into the bathtub and go in there. We tried everything. We put a potty in the bathtub, one with Elmo on it. We talked and explained. Nothing helped. Because he was holding it all the time and he was afraid to go in his underwear, he took his underwear off and would go naked around the house.

On one of those naked days Dan's friend James was supposed to come for a play date. James, I had heard from the teachers, was Dan's best friend. I spoke to his mom on the phone and she was happy to bring him to play. I tried to talk Dan into getting dressed, but he just would not. When James and his mom arrived, Dan was happily playing naked in the living room. I felt terrible, and started to explain, but James' mom just waved her hand and smiled. She said she went through this the year before with James. "He will get it soon, you know. It just seems like forever, but you will see."

With just a few words this woman whom I hardly knew had made me feel so much better about my life, about Dan, about everything.

The least pleasant part of Dan's being naked was that when he could not hold it anymore, the "number two" could be found everywhere: living room rug, toys, kitchen floor, just-changed-this-morning white sheets. Being a person who keeps the house clean all the time, I could not stand this. I was constantly cleaning up after him. I changed our sheets day after day and had to wash them in our tiny washer. If you walked into our apartment you would see them hanging around on the chairs because our washer was also the dryer. It took three days for a comforter cover to dry.

It was a nightmare. But I knew I had to stick with it just a little longer, and he would get it. And then my life would be different.

Outside the house it was even harder. At this point, with Dan not using diapers anymore, when we were out of the house for long periods of time, Dan would go in his underwear. I would have to take him to the bathroom and change all of his clothes.

I knew it was temporary, so I kept on sticking to the process. It became my lone project, because for some reason Alex could not deal with cleaning the poop.

One evening as Dan was still fighting pooping in the toilet, I hit my limit. I was bathing Gali in the spotlessly clean bathtub. I had cleaned the house that day, and Gali and I were having the best time. I was checking on Dan periodically. I knew he had to go because I could smell the releases of gas all that evening. (We moms have our ways of knowing when they really have to go.)

While Gali and I were laughing and singing with the rubber ducky, I suddenly heard a scream. It was not Dan's voice, which was a comfort for a moment. It was Alex. I ran to see what happened. I found Alex in the doorway still with his coat and his briefcase in his hand. He had walked in to find a poop storm. Dan had done his business in the hall and because he was embarrassed and scared, he tried to clean up. There was poop everywhere, on the door, on the shoes, on the clean sheets. And on his hands.

When I saw that, I could not take it anymore. I had been dealing with this for too long. It was just too much. What was I doing wrong? I had to clean the house all over again. I had to sanitize Dan somehow. I had to do all this while exhausted. I had to put my time with Gali aside again. It was not fair!

At that moment, I just lost it. I was so angry with Dan. I was angry with myself for letting him be there for more than three seconds without supervision. I was angry with Alex for not returning home five minutes earlier, to help prevent this. I was angry and I was sad. It was my turn to have a meltdown.

Alex and I worked very hard to clean the house that night. Many clothes and toys had to be thrown into the trash. We sanitized the floors. We washed the sheets. We were sweaty and tired and upset.

When we were done, and everything was clean, and the kids were finally asleep, we filled ourselves a warm bubbly bath and slipped into the water. We were emotionally drained. We were two people stretched beyond their abilities. Beyond anyone's ability. We just lay there and cried. The warm water and the lavender scented bubbles surrounded us and calmed our souls.

We held each other. When we were together like this I knew we could survive anything, even a poop storm.

Lucky for me the next day I was supposed to meet the other autism moms for lunch. I knew they would understand, so I told them everything. As I expected, my story opened the door for everyone else to tell their own poop horror stories. My friend Diana said that one day she's going to write a sequel to the book *Everybody Poops* by Taru Gomi. She is going to call it "Everybody has poop stories." While all parents have them, with autism the poop stories are just more extreme.

The next Monday, Dan did it. He went to the toilet on his own and pooped right in it. There was no limit to my joy and pride.

The next day I drove him to school and decided to make a big deal about it. I asked that they call Nancy, the teacher in charge of toilet training.

I said, "Nancy, Dan has something to tell you."

She bent down looked at Dan and asked him, "Dan, what do you have to tell me?"

Dan replied with three words: "I did it!"

LEARNING ABOUT THE SPIRITS

March 2009

During our next conversation, I asked Joseph what else Dan was "seeing" that was different.

"You mean the Spirits that take over?" said Joseph.

As soon as he said that my body shook with chills. I remembered my conversation with Dr. Nader from exactly a year earlier.

***

Dr. Nader is a respectable cardiologist in Israel, who is also a natural healer treating people with a unique method he invented. Amelia, who has been working closely with him, told me about his book, *Medicine and the Seventh Sense.*

When my stepchildren came to visit us in the summer of 2006, just after we moved to Connecticut, I asked them to bring me the book. It was filled with diagrams and complex explanations about physics and chemistry, that explained energy healing, and I was getting through it slowly.

One day Dan was playing in our bed around his naptime. I thought he was going to fall asleep so I stayed in the living room with the big kids. After a while I could still hear sounds, so I went to peek into the room. I walked in and saw Dan reading Dr. Nader's book. He was looking deeply into a page and looked like he was studying a diagram. I came closer and saw that a glass full of water that was on the bedside table was gone. Scared of the possibility of Dan getting cut, I looked around carefully. I looked down and saw that the glass dropped and was caught between the bedside table and the bed, still upright and full of water.

More than a year later, at yet another low point, we were going through all the changes in Dan's program and not sure what the best path was. Thanks to Amelia putting us together, I got to talk to Dr. Nader himself. I told Dr. Nader about Dan and what I had tried with him. I told him about Dan reading his book and what happened to the glass of water.

“Shirley,” he started, and I could hear in his voice that he was debating how much he could tell me, “you are dealing with something that is related to the world of the demons. Dan’s development is delayed because some of the time they take over him and it is like he is not here.”

Dr. Nader continued: “from what you are saying, I can tell that Dan can be a genius one day, if only someone can teach him the right way.”

It was the weirdest explanation accompanied by the most wonderful predication.

***

Now, more than a year after that conversation, I wanted to hear Joseph’s explanation of that idea. “The Spirits,” the way Joseph described them, were energies that were bothering Dan. They were negative energies that would ‘take over’ him. “When he is taken over by the spirits, it is like he is not here.”

“But how do they do that?”

“The spirits I am talking about are mean and very powerful. They make themselves look nice at first and they make Dan want to come to them. Then they take over."

"So it is like a demon?" I cringed, not liking the idea that what he said matched Dr. Nader's explanation.

"Exactly, but I do not like to call them that. To me they are spirits."

"And they look nice? How?" I did not completely get it.

"They can take any form they like. They can appear as a nice boy to play with. It is like when a puppy sees a snake. It wants to play with it and it doesn't know that the snake is dangerous."

Joseph explained that people like Dan and himself are very sensitive to the different energies out there. They are more aware, so they notice them. According to Joseph, the spirits were using Dan's body as an instrument to exist in the "physical world."

After we hung up the phone, I sat still for a while. I could not move. I needed to process what I had just learned. So Dan is "not here" some of the time. Sounds imaginary, yet I did feel it myself, that he was not present. Often he did not look me in the eye. That could be the explanation, as preposterous as it may seem. It was not as if I had any evidence to contradict what Joseph was saying. And he had been through autism and came out on the other side, free and healthy.

The healer in me wanted to believe. But then the lawyer in me intervened: This is completely insane. How desperate was I to accept this theory as true?

I had to go back to my basic rule: I was willing to learn everything and do anything, even if it seemed to not make sense, as long as it helped Dan.

I decided to watch and see if talking to Joseph indeed taught me something I could use on a practical level.

Joseph explained to me that in order for me to pull Dan into my world, I have to first make a step towards his world. "See where he is in the moment and join him," was his practical advice. "If you want him to talk to you, you need to learn how to talk to him, in his language, first. And that is what I am in the process of teaching you."

The next morning after the spirits conversation, I had an opportunity to test the practical aspect of what Joseph had been teaching me. Dan was in the midst of one of his tantrums. I knew what it was. He needed to go to the bathroom, but his body was not quite there yet, so he needed something to eat. He was hungry but he would not sit at the table. He could not tell me what he wanted to eat. He did not even look at what I offered him. He climbed onto the counters looking for food and then stared at the open fridge. And all this time he was whining loudly. Nothing I did would calm him down.

I cooked wagon wheels pasta, his favorite. At this point he was so frustrated, he went to our bedroom and was crying loudly in our bed. I brought the pasta to him. When I gave him the bowl, he started throwing the pieces of pasta over the headboard, one by one. Such annoying behavior would usually push me over the edge. It was frustrating enough to hear Dan's whining all morning and not be able to help him.

But then I remembered what Joseph and I talked about. Joseph said that I should join Dan in whatever he was doing, whether it was stimming or anything else, annoying as it might be. So that moment I decided to try. As Dan was throwing the pasta over the headboard and onto the floor, I reached into his bowl and took one piece. Dan stopped and looked at me. I was already not doing what he expected, which was to say 'no!' I took the piece and threw it over the headboard. He looked at me in shock. He took one more and threw it. I took one and threw it too. Before we started this, Dan was still whining. As soon as I threw the first piece of pasta, he stopped. He kept throwing the pieces behind the headboard, but he was quiet. After two exchanges of throwing pasta, Dan smiled. Soon after that he started to laugh. He completely forgot what made him uncomfortable. He was with me.

I tried it again later that week, when we got home from horseback riding. It was Friday evening and Dan was tired from the intensive school week, the long drive to the horses, and the riding itself. I could relate. I could not wait to go upstairs and relax. But then Dan refused to come out of the car. He put his foot up on the window, as if to say: "don't open the door, because I will kick you."

Remembering what Joseph said, I didn't open the door. I leaned over on the next car in the parking lot and I put my foot with my sole facing Dan's sole, with the closed window between us. I had to wait less than a minute before I saw Dan smiling. I opened the door and he gladly came with me.

THE DIMENSIONS

March 2009

It was time for me to complete Joseph's assignment and watch the movie "The Matrix."

Watching the film after having a few conversations with Joseph and acquiring a new level of understanding was amazing. I really got the message they were trying to convey, about the different levels of existence. They showed it very nicely in the film visually, the body being in one place and the mind operating separately and independently in another, creating a complete parallel life.

Then I watched "Bleep." This film included scientific evidence to support the theory that since the mind affects so much of what we do, we can create and control what happens to us. I knew this was possible, because it had happened to me in the past. Things that I wrote and focused on became real.

I once had a crush on a guy and I channeled my obsessive thoughts about him into writing. I had a friend who was studying film writing. I asked her to guide me in writing a script for a short film. The film was – of course – about a guy and a girl who were similar to me and the guy I was in love with. I left the end open, on purpose, because nothing was really happening between me and the guy, but then my friend who read the script for me said, "Oh, it is so obvious that they will fall in love." And indeed, after a while, that guy and I ended up being in a relationship. Whether this was my prayer being answered, or my being so focused on it, this happened in reality! Watching those two movies made me remember that.

I pondered it for a while. If that indeed was the case, and I created something I truly desired for myself in the past, what does it mean? Could I do it again? Could I make more things happen?

And then my mind went back to the scenes from "The Matrix." The two forms the people could move between: the world we "live" in, where their bodies were, and the world in their mind, where they could be only if they were connected to a special machine. What an incredible idea: Existence on more than one level.

I suddenly remembered something. A theory I had when I was a little girl, about the concept of time. How I thought that each moment in time never ceases to exist. How I pictured the 'me' of a minute ago still existing somewhere, and how the 'me' of a few minutes from now already exists, only I haven't gotten to 'her' yet. How the 'me' of all those moments of past and future exist at the same time.

And then my consciousness was absorbing something. Glimpses of understanding were making their way to me. The mind-body connection that I was so drawn towards was not the complete picture. It was more like mind-body-soul-universe-network of people. A very clear understanding washed over me: Dan, in that "other" form, completely free of autism, already exists. He is just in a different dimension. I could almost physically feel the membrane separating where he is now, and that other perfect existence. And at the same time I understood that it was reachable. There was a way to get there.

It was as if there were different levels - or dimensions - of existence. Those dimensions are parallel. While we lived in one of them, the others continued to exist. There are parallel universes and we exist in all of them at the same time. The interesting part was that I believed we could move between dimensions. While someone is in one dimension, they could choose, when the opportunity came, to step to a higher level. They could also step down. That was a choice they could make. And if they decided to go up, there would come another opportunity later that would enable them to choose again. If they stepped up again, they were getting closer to a higher level. Which meant that if one maintained focus and recognized when an opportunity came their way, they could make a change that would take them higher, until they actually move to the next dimension.

But what were those opportunities? I remembered reading in my healing books about the "lessons." Perhaps it is our lessons that give us a choice. Once an experience comes along, we have the option to learn from it and grow, or stay in our old beliefs and remain where we are. And when we choose to learn, we go higher.

So if for example, I was facing hardship with Dan, I could either spend my time hating it, or I could decide to take it as a lesson, learn it, and get past it. Because after all, that is what life is all about: Learning.

TAKE CARE OF YOURSELF

March 2009

In our next conversation, Joseph insisted that I needed to take care of myself. Lots of therapists say that. It's just like the airlines tell us: "Put your own oxygen mask on before you help others." Of course we mothers forget about that. We take care of everyone else and we are reminded of our needs only after we are breathless, lying on the floor crying somewhere. Maybe it *was* time to turn that around.

One of the things Joseph suggested was to go back to doing things I like. I had to take time to think. What did I like and feel like doing? Usually my idea of fun was good food and movies. I had these already. Too much of the first, unfortunately, and a bunch of the second, with my on-line movie rental membership.

There was the 20 pounds I needed to lose. I had been carrying them since Gali was born, which was around the time we got Dan's diagnosis.

Would I have lost them by now if I had not been submerged in the treatment of autism? Probably yes. Maybe this was a good place to start.

I remembered my friend told me about this exercise class she went to, called Zumba. She said it was better than an orgasm. (Well, she was in a sexless marriage approaching a divorce, so perhaps her description was not exactly true to life, but I was willing to give it a try.)

Good decision. Not good, great. When I came to the class there were so many women in the studio, some of them older ladies and some of them out of shape too. Then the instructor came in, a tiny, energetic blonde with a huge smile. She put the music on and to my amazement all of the women started to perform these Latin dance moves. Moving their arms, shaking their hips and their shoulders, at times looking like crazy chickens. Nobody cared how you looked, how old you were, or whether you could follow the moves correctly. Shortly after the class started, we were all sweaty and smiling from ear to ear.

When the class ended I noticed that this was the first time in a long while that I had been happy. I was not thinking about anything I needed to do. I was not thinking of the goals Dan had not met yet. I was not thinking of autism at all! I was not thinking of anything but the moment. It was easy. The music and the movement brought my mind into a calm place.

I signed up then and there as a member of the studio. Wow, if I could have even just an hour a week of absolute happiness, it was worth it.

When I went to another Zumba class, I realized that the more I danced with all those women having fun and no judgment, the more I remembered how much I liked to dance as a child. I've heard that it's good during a time of crisis to remember what you really liked to do as a child and then do it. It is supposed to take you to a good place inside yourself: a happy place.

I used to love to dance. Why did I ever stop doing that? And then I suddenly remembered a completely different dance class. It was when I was 11. I was too advanced for my ballet class, so they bumped me up to the next group with the older girls. There was a mean girl there that I remember to this day. At the first exercise when we were supposed to walk one by one across the room, she was walking behind me holding her leotard where her boobs should be, pulling it out. She was making fun of mine that were far too big for my age. Everybody laughed, and it made that class the last ballet class I ever took. I never told anybody why I stopped dancing and I had to listen to my mother's remarks every time we went to my sister's recitals about how I used to be the best dancer, better even than my sister, who was very gifted. Coming to Zumba class and feeling great about dancing again was a corrective emotional experience for me.

When I thought about dancing and working out I realized that it served much more than the purpose of losing weight. It also helped me feel better and stronger. And then it came to me that a person doesn't have to be that skinny to look good. Although I could not fit into any of my old clothes anymore, I was only one size bigger. My body was just a bit different now. There were ways to look better without losing it all. Look what they do in all those makeover TV shows. After they do a complete makeover on a girl, not only does she look more beautiful, her self-confidence is high and she is happier. All they've done is change her clothes and hair and makeup. Losing weight is not part of it.

I decided to not give up on that idea, but to try and see what else I could do. I decided I should go see my hairdresser more frequently. Once in six months for partial highlights and a trim did not do it. I also decided to think more about the way I dressed. Perhaps it was not a good idea to wear sweatpants and oversized t-shirts every day.

I opened the bathroom cabinet and looked at all my face cleaners and creams. I hadn't touched them in a while. The mornings were completely hectic getting Dan and Gali out the door, and at night I would fall asleep with the kids, too exhausted to do anything for myself. Yet, there was still plenty of time during the day when the kids were at school. I could clean my face and apply my creams in the middle of the day.

***

To this day, there are times when stress takes over and it's hard to find the time and energy to take care of myself. Days when even being able to take a long shower feels like a vacation. Days when I don't even think of applying makeup because I know I would cry in the car on my way home from driving Dan to school. Yet I make the effort to find those times, even if it's a few minutes just for me to do something nice, and it feels good and helps me keep going. As my husband Alex puts it: "You're no good to any of us if you don't take care of yourself. And you're the one who holds us all together. So go rest, work out, something!"

Blog Post from my website January 20, 2012:

Hair Trends for 2012 Perfect For Autism Moms

I looked at the on-line magazines before my last hair appointment to see what the trends are for hair in 2012.

I am happy to report that for the first time in fashion history the hair trends are perfectly appropriate and match the life-style of the classic autism mom.

Since you do not know, I will tell you – the new hot hairstyle is greasy at the top and messy on the bottom. Yes! Exactly what we needed: fashion is on our side!

Here is how you can achieve a salon look while maintaining your busy autism-mom-schedule:

You are woken up at 5 am by your child and she refuses to back to sleep? You turn your head on the pillow from side to side in disbelief that she is doing this to you AGAIN!?

Great, you are on your way to achieving your messy look.

You make the lunches and get your kids ready for

school. You leave without a chance to even brush your hair? Fantastic, you are one step closer.

You work, workout, do errands pick up the kids from school to bring them to their ABA/ speech therapy/ OT or what not? Great!

You are late for ABA and sweating with guilt in the waiting room? Awesome!

By the next morning – especially if you fell asleep in front of the TV and had no time or energy to shower – you will achieve the latest hair look for 2012: greasy at the top, messy on the bottom.

Congratulations!

CREATIVE IDEAS

April 2009

One day while driving I got a new great idea. What if I wrote a book? A book about Dan and me, and all the things I was learning thanks to him. Dan's condition made me think in different ways and working with Joseph helped me implement those ideas in my life. Writing would enable me to express my voice. What if this would later help Dan use his voice as well?

A few days later I got enough courage and told Alex about my idea.

He immediately turned away from me and went to our bedroom. He did not say a word. I followed him and saw him go online on our computer. He bought me a laptop - my own brand new laptop that I could use to write my stories.

Me. A writer. The thought made me so happy. I started writing about my meetings with my group of moms, about the things I was learning from Joseph, about things that happened at home.

While I was driving with Dan, I kept a notebook and whenever I got an idea for a story, I would pull over and write it down. The ideas started piling up, because interesting things were happening all the time.

For the first time in a while I felt like I was doing something meaningful, besides caring for Dan and the family.

I noticed that the more I wrote, the more ideas I was getting. Writing helped me feel better and make sense of everything that was happening with Dan. I was more focused and more aware.

I had a feeling that besides helping me deal with autism, my book could help others. I began to dream. What if my book was published and became a success? What if one day someone would be interested in making a film out of it, to share the insights and the optimism with all the other autism parents out there who were fighting for their lives, just like me?

The more I thought about all those autism parents out there, the more inspired I became.

One day I was dropping Dan off at school and I saw one of the moms dropping her daughter off. The little girl was just so beautiful. Suddenly a thought came to my mind.

What if a clothes designer would publish a catalog of his children's line and have children with autism as the models? Just one time, get the kids dressed in the designer's clothes and let them play and be photographed being their natural selves. Some of them will flap their arms, spin or just run, but a good photographer would be able to capture their good moments and their beauty. And then the world would see how beautiful they are. How they are not different from other children.

And now that I was thinking of it, what if there was a company that manufactured clothes especially for kids with autism? There would be no labels of course. The fabrics should be very soft and comfortable. Some of the clothes should be super light and loose because there are kids who cannot stand anything touching their skin. Others should be heavier and tight for kids like Dan who need deep pressure input. They could make shoes too. Shoes with springs on the bottom to give the kids the input of bouncing that so many of them seek. Or shoes that have weights on them, again, for that deep pressure input.

I got excited then. What if autism parents designed these clothes? There are hundreds of thousands of us, especially moms, staying at home, taking care of the kids. Most of the day we are busy with them, but during the few extra hours we have, what if we channeled the energy to making something instead of worrying? There have to be photographers and designers among us. Engineers, marketing specialists, and what not. All we need is to get together and take positive actions.

It takes a village to raise a child and in our case help him get well. Why can't we create a village to help ourselves?

***

When the movie Tangled came out and I was watching it over and over with Gali, I could not help but think as Rapunzel was singing: "when will my life begin?" And so many of the moms I got to know through working in my organization *Autism Parents Community* were asking the same question. So many of us could not possibly go to work because straight from school we would drive the kids to therapy, and there was no guarantee how our kids would be doing at school and when we would have to be there for them. Even if they worked, most moms still felt trapped, because they could never take the kids with them anywhere. Vacations or even trips to a store were not an option. Just like the blonde Disney princess, we were all wondering, when will our life begin?

I later got to think more about this concept. If it wasn't for Dan and his challenge, I would not have written this book, because I wouldn't have gone on this journey in the first place.

***

Returning to March 2009, I finally got to watch the third movie I rented. It was a film with many familiar actors in it, that's why I picked it.

As it started and I was making myself comfortable on the sofa, I noticed a familiar face. It was one of the actors. He looked really familiar. Where had I seen him before? And then it hit me. He was a dad from Dan's school.

I suddenly remembered seeing him at the open house when Dan started going to Good School. He seemed familiar back then too. He smiled at me and I was not sure where I had seen him. I remember trying to think where in town I had met him. How embarrassing. Hc must have seen the look on my face.

But then, wait. This meant that I knew a real movie star. And was I not thinking of making my book, once I finished it, into a film? Maybe he could help me. He would have knowledge of how the industry works. I decided to not tell anyone yet, not even Alex, about my plan to talk to him. It would be my secret until it actually happened.

AUTISM AND MARRIAGE

April 2009

With all the uncertainty and disruption and trauma, it's not that surprising that the divorce rate in autism families is 80%.

Autism complicates a marriage. Picture the routine that a couple gets into after being married for a while. Then add the birth of a child. Now add autism. Then add a ton of worries related to the challenges of autism, together with uncertainty about how to help your child. On top of that add two tons of financial hardship caused by the expensive therapies and treatments. What do you get? Tough times.

Alex had been complaining a lot. About things that were not autism. The things that bothered him were real, yet I couldn't see how he could focus on them when we were dealing with something so big and important.

One day I got really angry with him.

“I can’t listen to this anymore. Do you even hear yourself?” I said to Alex when he started to talk about something related to his work again.

“You can’t listen because you don’t know what it’s like.”

“I’ve worked in the past. I know exactly what it’s like.”

“Then maybe you don’t remember. It’s been a while.”

“What are you saying?”

“I’m saying that you should appreciate what I’m doing.”

“What *you’re* doing?”

“Yes, earning a living. Which is something you don’t appreciate.”

“What about what *I’m* doing? Can’t you see that?”

"Yes, I can. But you don't have to do *so* much and you know it."

"What?" I got so angry at this point. "Can't you see I'm saving his life?"

"You are. But there is a price and you're ignoring it."

"Price?..." I said, sobbing at this point. "I don't care about the price."

"But I do. The reason I can't have a conversation with you is because anything that's not autism doesn't count anymore. We used to talk," he said, coming to sit next to me. "We used to have fun." He held my hand. "Now it's all fear and work and sadness. Not only am I losing my boy to autism, I'm losing you too."

After that day we made a new rule. Once a week we would go out to dinner. We made an arrangement with our babysitter that in addition to the days she came to help me after school, we would have her come every Saturday night, so Alex and I could go out.

The first few times, I fell asleep during dinner. Later I managed to make it through the whole dinner and only fell asleep in the car on the way home. The more we did it, the better our conversations became. And sometimes I even managed to truly enjoy a conversation that was not all about autism.

On our anniversary, I decided to plan a small celebration. We used to love to celebrate things. It was so much easier before autism came. Now at every celebration, whether it was a birthday – especially Dan's – or any other, we could not stop thinking about how much better things could have been if only we did not have autism in our life.

But we had to keep trying to be happy.

I decided to surprise Alex and have a Mexican night, so we could remember our amazing honeymoon in Mexico.

I prepared for it all week. I got Mexican decorations and hid them. I got tortilla chips and salsa and made guacamole. I was planning on making a full blender of frozen margaritas. It used to be my specialty when I lived in New York City.

I was waiting for Alex to come home from work, so we could celebrate. We would have the food with the kids, except for the margaritas, of course. Those were just for us. The second part of the plan was to "be together." We liked to call it that when the kids were around. We did not want either of them to repeat the word 'sex' to other people.

Making the margaritas involved some noise making. As I was turning the blender on, Dan, who could not stand loud noises, started banging his head on the floor. His sensitivity to sound had gotten so much better at this point, but he still needed physical comfort to handle such a loud sound and I had to be in the kitchen. I really wanted Alex to enjoy the surprise and for everything to be ready as soon as he walked in, so I figured a little quick noise would not be too bad.

I was wrong. Dan was tired and the noise was way too much for him to handle. This was one big tantrum. The head banging continued and Gali, who was scared by it, clung to me, screaming. I had two screaming children. There is an anniversary surprise for you!

By the time Alex came in, they were both fine. We had our dinner. Quick but still fun. The margaritas were the best part.

We bathed the kids together and put them to bed.

It was now our time to 'be together,' and Alex was not going to pass on the opportunity. You need to understand this. As a morning person, one who wakes up at 5 a.m. no less, sex after 9 p.m., actually any activity after that hour, was pretty much impossible. But I made an effort to stick to the plan.

We closed their room doors firmly. We lay a blanket on the living room rug. Sex in our comfortable king size bed was not possible, because Dan slept there. We had to compromise yet again. We started kissing. Hmmm, the taste of the sweet margaritas combined with the salty food was great. Our bodies felt relaxed from the alcohol. I felt like I was melting into him. His strong arms holding me. Images from our romantic vacation in Mexico came to my mind. The white beautiful sand. The turquoise water. The music. The food. The feeling of freedom. I let all this get to me. Wonderful together time.

Then we really got going and while rolling around on the rug my head found itself next to the coffee table. We kept going and my head was hitting the table.

Before I knew it, my thoughts about white beaches and turquoise water disappeared and instead I remembered only one image: our little boy helplessly banging his head on the floor.

***

As years go by we make an effort to preserve the special relationship we have. When we feel like the pressure and the stress is about to crush us, we try to remember everything we love about each other.

Because autism makes you forget who *you* are, it also makes you blind to the people around you. You forget what your life was like before. You forget how your husband was before. All you see is the miserable *now*.

Alex and I slowly learned to balance each other. I still have the drive to do more treatments and therapy all the time, and Alex balances me out by making me find out whether it would really be helpful and whether the time and money are worth the benefit Dan would be getting.

GOOD NEWS

May 2009

During Dan's first year at Good School, he progressed nicely. In the spring of that year, we realized that although he'd made great strides, Dan was not even close to being ready to be mainstreamed. We wanted him to continue his progress at Good School, but we could no longer afford it.

Like many other autism parents, we hired a lawyer. We decided to contact our school district and have them pay for Dan's placement at Good School. This can be done in cases where the public school doesn't have an appropriate program for the child, which we had been told was the case in our town.

The attorney we hired suggested that we get an evaluation done privately that would recommend the appropriate program for Dan. The plan was to then request a PPT, planning and placement meeting, after which the school district would perform its own evaluation and recommend a program for the child within the public school. Our attorney explained to us that it was likely that the program our district would offer us would not fulfill Dan's needs. Then it would be our turn to refuse it and demand that they place Dan at Good School and pay for it.

My friend Michelle recommended Dr. Berger to us for the evaluation. She told me that Dr. Berger was the toughest yet the sharpest psychologist in our area.

"I went to see her thinking my daughter was here," she said holding her hand at shoulder height, "and she told me she was here," she held her hand at her knee. "You may be crushed, but you know that whatever she is telling you is true."

Dan and I spent a whole day of testing at Dr. Berger's office. After that, Dr. Berger had a long talk with me asking many questions about Dan's development and current level of skills. During that questioning, I could hear in her voice that I was going to get exactly what Michelle got from her, if not worse. I could not stop thinking how Michelle held her hand high and then at her knee when she described how the results from Dr. Berger were so different from her expectations.

When it was time for me to go see Dr. Berger to receive the results, I was very nervous. Alex could not join me because Gali was home sick. There was no question that between the two of us, I should be the one to go. But the thought of getting thc bad news I was expecting all by myself was dreadful.

I decided to take my laptop and spend a short while writing at my favorite café before the appointment. By that time, writing was a therapeutic experience for me. It helped me see things clearly, it helped me deal with challenges, and it made me calm.

As I got downstairs to the lobby of our apartment building I noticed the most beautiful flower arrangement. They always had beautiful flowers in the lobby, but this one was exceptional: beautiful huge peonies in all shades of pink: gentle baby pink, fuchsia, and my favorite, the full body pink that only peonies come in. I stopped to smell the flowers, closed my eyes and felt the fluffiness of the petals against my skin. I inhaled the intoxicating scent and felt like I was in a sun-washed field, warmed by the sun.

After getting my coffee and finding a spot at the café, I had exactly twenty three minutes left to write. I decided to spend this time writing a future scene in my book. I wanted it to be a really positive one, about how Dan would be when he is better, when he has overcome his challenges.

There is a famous deceased rabbi – Rabbi Nachman – who used to teach his students that a person exists where their thoughts are. I decided to form my thoughts into the best ones I could at that moment. I got to write a page and a half and then it was time to go. I packed my laptop and got into the car. I knew I was as ready to receive the news as I would ever be.

I walked into Dr. Berger's clinic and sat on the couch. Dr. Berger was smiling at me as she was gathering her papers and opening Dan's file. The whole life of a child, of a family, folded in those pieces of paper. Our life.

I could not wait for her to tell me already. Whatever it was I suddenly needed to just hear it, get it over with.

"Good news."

What? What did she just say? Is she talking to me?

"Good news," she said again after seeing the puzzled look on my face.

Apparently, between the time she saw Dan at her clinic and had the milestones-conversation with me, the same conversation that gave me the bad post-evaluation feeling, she had gone to see Dan at Good School.

She was impressed with how well the teachers have been working with him there. She said they were great, knew what they were doing, knew Dan very well and knew how to handle him, even when he had a hard time.

"When they were working with him I could see Dan's potential," she said. "I saw how much they could get out of him there. You know that you will see the progress first in therapy and then in real life."

Wow, Dan was starting to show his potential in therapy. He did well. I could not believe my ears. This woman, who was the smartest and sharpest psychologist in Connecticut, was giving me good news! Of course there was still a long way to go, he is not where other kids his age are, they are already having sleepovers at this age - why is everyone always worried about sleepovers? - Yet there is hope. And we are on the right track.

I left the office and felt like I was on a cloud. My heart was about to burst. I could not wait to get home and tell Alex what she had said word by word. Since I have always been overly optimistic - is there such a thing? - he would not believe me if I just said, “Oh, it went well, there is hope.” He needed the actual words from the person, to make sure it was not my special pink-glasses-translation.

As soon as I drove out of the clinic’s parking lot, on my way home, I noticed them. They were placed on a cart on the sidewalk: Beautiful bouquets of peonies, in all shades of pink. I stopped the car and went to look at them. They were arranged in little vases and there was a note that said how much they cost, with a box to put your money. The note was signed “the flower lady.”

It was completely magical: A cart of beauty in the middle of the street, with my favorite flowers, in pink, after I got such good news. I am always out of cash when I need it, but I managed to find enough coins in the car to bring one bouquet home. They smelled so wonderful. And even more importantly, they were a sign: A sign of hope.

FEARS

May 2009

During our next conversation Joseph and I talked about fears. “What are you afraid of, Shirley?”

“Right now I am afraid of those crazy spirits you told me about and all those energies surrounding Dan.”

“Why are they scaring you?”

“Because I cannot see them and I am afraid of what they can do to Dan.”

“What else are you afraid of?”

I had to think for a minute. What *was* I afraid of?

“That Dan will not be OK, that he will always have autism, despite all the things we are doing to try and save him.”

"And what scares you about that?"

"That he will end up alone. One day we will not be here for him. With him."

"I think it is time you let go of that fear."

"How can I do that?"

"You know how you are always surrounded by people?"

"Yes," I was not sure where he was taking this.

"Remember how you told me about this pattern you have of getting very close to people and then leaving them because something happens?"

"Yes."

"Why do you think that happens?"

"Why what do you mean?"

"I mean why do those relationships end up being that way?"

"Because people disappoint me. I put so much effort into my relationships, and then people don't reciprocate."

"And why do you put so much effort into those relationships? You have a family that loves you and a husband who adores you, yet you are still looking to get more. More what? Attention? Love?"

"I just need people around me."

"Because...." He waited.

"Because I don't want to be without people."

"Because I'm afraid of...." He waited again.

"Being alone," I finally said quietly.

"Do you remember what you told me in the beginning of our conversation? What's your biggest fear about Dan?"

"Yes," I said quietly. "I think I am reflecting my own fears on him."

"People do that all the time. The difference is that you are brave enough to increase your awareness and see the truth. That's really amazing."

I reviewed what he had said in my mind quietly and he continued.

"As for your other fear, of the beings and the energies," he said. "Your fear of them is actually an opportunity. The energies are fighting for your attention. They are taking over Dan and then you are actually 'communicating' with them instead of him."

"Oh no!"

"That's OK. It doesn't hurt him. If you want the energies to go away you need to be direct. Do not play around with them. Be firm. Create boundaries. They will end up leaving."

"Be direct..." I tasted the words slowly. "Not be afraid of what they think of me."

"Exactly," he said, happy that I made the connection between my own two biggest fears. "You know, Shirley," Joseph continued, "fears are negative energy that is blocking your channel. Once you let go of your fears, you will be making room for positive things to come your way."

Next Joseph asked me about Dan's fears. Dan had a fear of water. He was so scared of water that he could not take a bath. We showered him with a cup, standing up in the bathtub. We had to stop and turn off the water when the water level in the bathtub was over an inch.

What if there was something I could do to help Dan get over this fear? What if after he got over it, it would waste so much energy on the fear, would he be able to learn more and just be happier?

I met the moms for lunch and talked to them about it. Bridget told me about this amazing swim teacher who specialized in special needs kids. "If you do that with her, she will find a way to get Dan in the water, and even teach him how safe it can be and that he can move his body to stay in it by himself." What a great idea. I called the teacher and went to see the pool she worked at.

I arrived at a big indoor town pool. It was huge and the acoustics were terrible. It was also humid and the odor from the chlorine was hard to take. I knew I would not be able to get Dan past the door here. I had to find another solution.

I called the teacher and asked her if she was teaching anywhere else. "Dan would not go in there. I need to find a smaller and quieter pool to do this." She said she will check but she was not very optimistic. She suggested I ask around to see whether I knew someone with a pool so she could come to us.

That weekend Dan was invited to the birthday party of a boy from school. Just like that first birthday where we all met, the parents learned the trick of sending the invitations to school to put in all the kids' backpacks. It was not like we could ask our kids who they played with at school. Our kids were non-verbal.

When Dan and I arrived at the birthday party I immediately spotted Gina with her son, Evan. She was by far one of my favorite moms. She was into energy healing and completely spoke "my language." At this point in my life the world was divided into "those who spoke my language" and those who didn't.

I saw her standing at the opening of the inflatable castle trying to see if Evan and his two brothers were OK. 'How lucky that they even go in there,' I thought. Dan could never take the noise of the pump that keeps it inflated, so although he loved bouncing he could never enjoy those toys.

"What's up?" she asked after we hugged.

"Nothing much," I said. "I spent my week looking for a swimming solution for Dan. He is afraid of water and I think it is blocking him energetically." 'Thank God I found someone who understands it that way at this party,' I thought. "I found a special needs swim teacher but the pool is awful: Big and loud and not fun at all. I want to find a small quiet pool for him."

"Bring him to our pool," she said immediately. "We just built it last year. Evan loves it. He won't come out of the water for hours. We would love to have Dan come any time you want."

I could not believe my ears. We had never been to their house, so I had no idea they had a pool. The first person I talk to about this dilemma and she has a pool and invited us over! I was really touched by how sweet Gina was. She was the mother of triplets. She had three boys, one of them on the autism spectrum. She was a teacher working fulltime. She kept her spirit up and shut off anyone who tried to judge her. When the moms met one time, she told us how once Evan was lying on the floor at the store and refused to move. She was there with him and his two brothers and was busy paying for their stuff. The lady standing behind her in the line looked at Evan screaming on the floor and then gave Gina a look and blurted something offensive. Gina turned around to face her, looked her in the eye and said: "Don't judge me. You don't know my story!"

At the birthday party Gina and I shook hands. The deal was that Dan and I would come to their pool once a week, and in return I would do my energy healing with her and with Evan.

I was looking forward to doing healing for Gina. I was also confident that I could help Evan.

Just the week before the party I got a confirmation of my energy healing abilities. I ran into my friend Dena downtown and we sat and talked. She told me something I did not know that showed me my potential: In the winter of 2008, when I was just playing with the idea of practicing energy healing with kids on the autism spectrum, I was with the kids at this big playdate at Gali's friend's house. My friend Dena was there too with her daughter Mia who also has autism. I decided to practice so I asked Dena if I could talk to Mia. Dena just laughed and waived her hand in disbelief. She did not see how anyone could engage Mia in that busy environment. I sat by Mia on the floor and telepathically asked her "Mia, how can I help you? Show me something, please." I concentrated and suddenly a picture of a heavy metal door came to my mind. Mia was still doing the same thing she was doing, but her subconscious was communicating with me, I was sure. She was trying to tell me something.

But then came doubt. Anyone knows that autistic kids feel trapped, naturally trapped can mean behind a door. But then here we were, Dena and I, more than a year after that playdate, sitting for coffee. I was obsessed with Dan's fear of water so I told her about it too. And then she told me about Mia's fear: doors. My heart stopped and I felt chills down my back. I told Dena what Mia "showed" me during our "conversation." "Yeah, she is terrified. She won't leave her room on her own. She won't leave the house unless we carry her over the threshold. When we come to a new place she won't go in. We have to carry her in our arms, and she is big, you have seen her, and she shakes and screams the whole time. Once she is in, she is fine. But getting her over a door step is a nightmare."

That week I kept thinking about how I could do great things for our kids. I can listen to them. I can understand them. This was probably why I offered my help to Gina so naturally when she offered her pool to us. I knew I could help her son.

SURRENDER

May 2009

When Dan and I came to Gina's pool, we were delighted. We walked in through their spacious backyard. They had a huge lawn and a big swing set. We entered through the gate to find a beautiful, clean light blue pool. The clear water sparkled in the sun. Their many toys lying around and floating in the water added colorful decorations to the lovely picture we already saw.

Evan was already in the water when we arrived. I jumped right in, and tried to convince Dan to join me. He didn't. All during our visit there he did not get his feet even close to the water. But he did find another way to have fun. He enjoyed throwing things into the water. Evan's two typical brothers came in and out of the pool all the time and were throwing toys to Dan, waiting for him to throw the toys back at them in the water. It was a hot day and the pool was perfect. Dan playing with the other two boys enabled me to find some alone time with Evan to see if I could practice natural healing the way I had learned from Joseph.

The more I tried the more frustrated I got. Evan completely blocked me. If I followed Joseph's energies explanation, the spirits did not let go of Evan the whole time I was there. The whole time he was scripting (repeating parts of stories and TV shows). He was not looking at me at all. He was this beautiful, sweet boy captured by something. It was so sad. And then I became angry. It was not fair! Why did this happen to him? Why was this beautiful boy trapped like that?

When Dan and I got into the car I could already tell I had gotten sunburned. With my pale skin it happened to me a lot, especially in the beginning of the season. But this one was quite severe and painful. When we arrived home I applied all the creams I could find in the house. Alex later went to the pharmacy to get me something stronger. It took many days for my skin to heal.

When I talked to Joseph that week and told him about my burn, he asked me, "What are you fighting?"

He then explained to me that there was a connection between those events: my frustration with Evan and my sunburn and pain.

He gave me an assignment for the week: surrender.

"What?"

"It means to not get emotionally involved. If you hear a child scream, do not pity him. If Alex is complaining about something, do not to try and understand him. Let people go about their business without getting involved. It is theirs, not yours.

"The next step will be to practice that same thing with the spirits. If you do not pay attention to them, do not indulge them, find a way to move yourself away from them, they would eventually go and leave Dan."

JOSEPH'S WARNING

May 2009

Alex and I made plans to go away. My mom came all the way from Israel to help us and stay with the kids, with the help of our babysitter Dara.

I was looking forward to some nights where I would not have to think about who would wake me up early this time and whether I would be lucky enough to sleep till 5 a.m. I also would not have to fall asleep at 8 with Dan in our bed. My mom and Dara would do it, for whole three nights.

I was also delighted to have time by myself with Alex. I was hoping that while Alex and I were relaxing on the beach or the pool, I would be able to talk to him a little bit about exactly what it was that I was doing with Joseph. Alex and I were constantly talking about Dan's progress and about our financial challenges, but we never got to talk about the depth of the process I was going through. I felt like I wanted him to understand some of it.

During one of our sessions, Joseph had asked me about Alex and how he was taking the autism situation. I knew where he was going with this. If both parents were to go through a "progression," as he called it, things would work out better for Dan, but I had very little hope that Alex would ever participate in anything like the things Joseph and I had been talking about.

Alex was supportive of my work with Joseph, because he knew I was not going too crazy with it and apart from burning some weird powders and talking about weird stuff behind closed doors, nothing much had changed. He also noticed that in general working with Joseph put me in a good mood and positive attitude, so he was fine with it. But actively participating in such work did not seem possible.

One of the things Joseph noticed when he was asking me about Alex was how stressed out Alex was. Between working so hard, commuting, having to pay the enormous tuition and having kids from a previous marriage living away from him, it was easy to guess that he was stressed out, but Joseph was noticing something more. He noticed that Alex never let himself really deal with what Dan's autism meant for him. He was dealing with the practical side of what he needed to do to help Dan, but he never dealt with the feelings he had about it. Of course there was the fear of "what will happen if..." But other than that, Alex never dealt with it. With the pain.

Joseph had a list of suggestions for Alex, like to write about it, or talk to a close friend, or go to the beach and go swimming and then write what he was feeling. The one suggestion that made me laugh out loud was to go and watch dolphins in the wild. Where the hell was I going to find dolphins here? There were those tours to see whales in Boston, but that was a two-hour drive each way. I shelved the idea until someday we could go on a trip there with the whole family.

When we started planning our trip, we decided on Mexico. This has always been our favorite vacation destination. When I spoke about it with Joseph a few weeks before booking the tickets he asked me not to do that. I asked why and he said he felt it would not be good. He had no real explanation for his feeling but he really insisted we not go there. It took me two whole weeks to decide what to do. I really wanted to go to Mexico. I kept on talking about it with Alex. He told me the decision was mine.

Since I'd been working with Joseph for a while now I knew that sometimes it was hard for me to understand at first where he was going with things but after a while his advice would make sense. Usually what he told me to do paid off and took me to a better place. After analyzing a bit more and obsessing about it on the phone with my mom, I booked us tickets to Key West instead.

Three days after I booked the tickets and the hotel I heard on the news about the swine flu spreading in Mexico. Many people in many places were affected. Some of them had died. The U.S. government recommended that Americans not go to Mexico. All the flights were cancelled. Everyone was terrified of the flu. It looked as though Joseph had been right again.

MY MOM

May 2009

The week before my mom came to visit, my entire session with Joseph was about her. It just happened. We did not discuss my assignments, he did not teach me anything new. Or at least that is how I saw it at the time. I was yet to learn how important that session was, and how far it would take me in my process.

Let me tell you a little bit about my mother. She and my dad got married when she was 24, soon after she graduated from Tel Aviv University and became a CPA. They had me, their first baby, a year later. My mom worked full time all her professional life in a management position at a large bank in Tel Aviv. She took her maternity leaves but would always go back to her job while raising her three girls and always being there for us. Of course she also made sure to maintain our beautiful house, and host fancy dinners that she cooked herself. She cooks wonderfully and is a great baker.

When I became a young woman it just happened that I followed in my mother's footsteps. The plan for me was to go to the university, acquire a good profession, get married, buy a house and have children. Just like my mother did.

When I was 24, it seemed like I was doing it all just right. I was in my second year of law school, well on my way to becoming a lawyer, I was married to my boyfriend of five years, and it seemed like I was on track to achieving all of my parents' expectations.

Three years after that I changed directions. I left my husband, put our new apartment on the market, and went to New York City to further my legal education. My ex husband and I had different ideas about what an ideal relationship was. While I thought that he was always too busy to spend time with me, he would say, "you just want a husband who comes home from work early and sits with you on the sofa while holding hands." I did need someone who would be focused on me and so I left.

When I moved to New York to pursue a masters in law, which would make me even more educated, improve my English and give me a better professional edge, my mom was still OK with it.

But when I decided to stay in New York and work at a law firm, my mom became uncomfortable. Time was passing by and I was still single. Career was important, yes, but she worried about my personal life. There was a husband, a house and kids in the plan for me.

When I met Alex that year and we got married a year later, she was happy. Now I was back on track to fulfill her plans for me. And when I got pregnant, she was delighted. Now I was doing it right! I had a position in a law firm in New York *and* I was heading towards having a family.

But then came autism.

At first, my mom did not believe the doctors. "I am looking at Dan's pictures right now and he is looking straight into the camera," she said to me on the phone, "Why do they say he has no eye contact?" It was true. Dan used to have eye contact and then he lost it after he got sick.

The more we learned, the better my mom got at understanding the magnitude of autism and how it affected my life. I could not go back to working as a lawyer and I focused my whole life on saving Dan. I had no job; I barely had friends; I had no plan for how to get my life together; and the worst part was I did not care. All I could see before me was my little boy who needed me.

My mom believed that I needed to stop all that. "You don't have a life anymore," she would often say. It was true. I had completely bailed on "the plan."

My mom and I talked on the phone a few times during the week before her scheduled flight. It was when I was still debating whether I should indeed give up the idea of going to Mexico, like Joseph insisted.

When she heard the news about the swine flu, she immediately called me. "How did Joseph know?"

My mom did not approve of my work with Joseph. She couldn't understand anything I told her about it. She rejected all the ideas of energies and spirits. I must say on her behalf that she was helping me fund it, which was what made it possible. This funding was due to my dad's belief that we should do absolutely anything to try and help Dan.

My mom's approach to spiritual people was the classic double standard. She behaved as if she didn't believe any of it and was actually appalled by such people. But when she was facing a problem, she would secretly go to see this rabbi or that psychic, "because it couldn't hurt."

When Joseph first heard that she was coming to visit, he was delighted and prepared a package for me. He sent us a picture to hang in the living room "with good energy in it." He sent me the "Zohar" books, that were used to practice Kabala, and promised to teach me how to use those soon. Lastly, he sent me a collection of powders I was supposed to burn in the apartment, to clear bad energy.

The closer it came to my mother's arrival the more nervous I got. Visits from my parents were extremely stressful as it was. For one thing, it meant a change of routine for Dan. He was usually very happy when they arrived, but then would get more stressed the longer they stayed. Perhaps this was because I was stressing out trying to make everyone happy. I was always busy and exhausted, between my parents wanting to see places, my mom wanting to go shopping and other family members coming to see us.

A bigger thing for me was that I was always nervous about how they saw Dan. Not seeing Dan for a while was a chance for them to see how far he had come, and I was always hoping for compliments. However, because of the distance between visits in combination with my parents' own denial, I was always bound to be disappointed. They would always question his progress and end up saying, "But he was always like this." Months of therapy and a million skills acquired didn't matter. But I always hoped that on the next visit things would be different.

Another thing was that my mom did not hesitate to express her opinions about my choices. One of her big things was that we needed to go back to living in Israel.

As much as she initially supported my life in New York, after Dan was born my mom's opinions completely shifted. She wanted me to come home. I am not sure whether it was because she saw how lonely I was in New York, being the only one among my friends having a baby, or whether it was that she knew how hard it is to raise a baby alone. My mom was away from her mother, my sweet loving grandma, when she had me and my one-year-younger sister. She and my dad lived a 3 hours' flight away from my grandparents, but they returned after the project my dad was involved with was over. It could also be that she missed Dan and wanted to be a bigger part of his life.

When we got Dan's diagnosis, and I sank deep into figuring out the right treatment and the right program for him, it became even harder for my mom to understand. She could get that the best schools and therapy were in America but she could not get why we needed to go through this alone. She had a point, but since Alex and I believed this was all temporary, and that with the right school and the right therapy it would be over, we could not see the point in moving back. Alex wanted to advance his career, and I wanted to stick to the plan. Dan would go to the best school, and within a year or two this whole autism thing would go away and we could go back to our old routine. We would visit Israel twice a year, and see everyone, and still keep our American lifestyle, which for us meant a more relaxed life than we would have in Israel.

My mom could not understand the difference in lifestyles and why we needed to stay away. For her it was simple: You have a family, you belong somewhere, and you should stay there.

The year before when she had visited, we argued about it. I told her how Alex really liked working here and the kind of people he was interacting with in the academic world. Her reaction was, "So you are here with no job and no life so Alex can enjoy his conversations at work?"

I felt like whatever I said didn't make sense to her – there had to be a really good reason to be away from home, right? - So I decided to blame it on Dan. "We simply cannot move him at this fragile point and the best therapy is here in America." My mom appeared to let it go. But she didn't completely, though. Since that visit, she talked about it with me during our many phone conversations. What were my professional plans, she wanted to know. At that time I was trying to build a healing practice, after I got my Bach Flowers Therapy education, and I had some workshops and some clients so she let go and waited to see how that played out before attacking the subject again.

I could see why it was hard for my mom to see me like this: not taking care of myself and not following the plan. But I couldn't figure out how I could explain myself to her.

During my conversation with Joseph, he told me that he thought that underneath all of my mom's "complaints," she really admired me. He said she thought I was so brave and that I was doing things she never dared to do. She was expressing her own fears when she complained about my choices. She wanted me, her daughter, to have the same accomplishments she had. It was a legacy. A legacy of "doing things right." There was not too much freedom there, not much choice. You could choose your profession and your husband, but not much more than that. Minding that list, it was hard to do anything innovative.

"You, on the other hand, are doing the opposite," said Joseph. "You live away from your family and don't have a 'proper' job. You have started to develop your natural healing practice. Your mom cannot understand why someone would do that. She thinks that because you stepped outside of the box, you will fail."

The day after my mom arrived I had another session with Joseph scheduled. He asked how it was when she came and I said fine. "Are you ready for something different today?"

"Yes."

"I was hoping you could work through things with your mom this visit."

"But there is nothing to really work on. We have disagreements but everyone does. It is completely unrelated to our work together. How is this related to Dan?"

"Oh. It actually *is* related. Because anything you are holding on to in your space that is not pure affects your ability to help Dan. What seems like 'almost nothing' to you may be big and painful for him. Plus, it's not really 'almost nothing' for you."

"OK. What do you need me to do?"

"Go to the other room to see your mom and put me on speaker."

Ugh, was he serious?

"Yes, I am serious," he said, reading my mind.

I went to the other room and told my mom I wanted her to participate in our talk. She agreed.

"Hello Tamar. It is nice to meet you."

"Hello," she said, completely uncomfortable, "You too."

"Shirley, tell your mother thank you and that you are sorry."

What?

"Tell her."

All of a sudden, out of nowhere, I started to cry. I don't know why I got so emotional. Somehow I mumbled, "Thank you and I am sorry."

"Sorry for what?"

"Tell her why. Tell her why you are sorry."

At first, I did not know. I was digging in me for the answer. Joseph and I had just talked about this, hadn't we? "For doing things differently," I finally said, "For doing things you do not understand, things you do not approve of."

Was this *me* talking? I felt like I was on that rollercoaster again, not knowing where my own thoughts and my own words would take me.

"For going away from you and staying away," I continued.

Now it was her turn to start crying. My mom has always been the emotional type. She cannot stand to see another person cry. Whenever anyone cried in her presence she would immediately start to cry too. What had I done, making my own loving mother cry? How must she be feeling seeing me suffer over Dan's situation for so long? And now I had made her cry on the phone with a stranger.

"But why are you doing this?"

"Because it is too loud for me in Israel."

"So we will find you a house in the country. You will be close to us and you will have your peace, nature, everything you want."

"But it is not about that. It is not only about not being in a city. It is the noise around me."

Now it was Joseph's turn to help me explain. "Tamar, what Shirley is talking about is an energetic-noise. I understand this. I feel it too. And for Dan it is better to stay away from it, for now."

Joseph was an expert on autism: he had it himself. My mom could not argue with that.

"Now, Shirley, tell your mom what you want her to do."

That rollercoaster again. What *did* I want her to do? And then it came to me.

"I want you to let go. Let me make my own choices and trust I know what is good for me." I was bawling now, could barely say the words, but she heard me.

"But you are throwing your life away," she wouldn't give up. "You are here all alone. You have not worked in God knows how long. All for Alex's job and dreams. What would happen if God forbid you were not with Alex anymore? If something happened to him? You are putting your life at stake."

So that's it? Just old fashioned parental worrying? She has been watching me drown trying to help Dan, and she wanted to help me. I realized that she couldn't help me. I had to find my own way. This was a territory she did not know. Everyone's life is different and generally parents can't always understand their kids and their choices, but my world was even more complicated. I was dealing with autism, something she could never understand. I truly respected all those worries about Alex and my relationship and my financial independence, but those concerns didn't even scratch the surface of my world. Regular people could spend time worrying about that. I simply couldn't. I had a son to save and he needed all of me to be focused on him. Whether I eventually had a life or not and who would be in it was not relevant. But how do I explain that to someone who had three healthy children, even if she was my mother? I couldn't, because she would never understand.

I suddenly felt a wave of warmth towards this loving woman. I understood now how different our lives had become as soon as I entered the world of autism. I understood now on a much deeper level that she would never understand my choices, because she did not speak this language. She was an autism grandma but that was very different from an autism mom.

"But Mom, you taught me that children come first no matter what," I said. "I am practicing what you have always shown me. My child is different and so my life is different. Trust me. I know what I am doing. You can let go."

"If that is what you want," she said slowly and quietly, "I will let you go."

And unbelievably enough, after that conversation, she did.

The next time I spoke to Joseph was after my mom left.

"I was applauding you," he said. "Do you know how much courage was required to do what you did with your mom? Some people take a lifetime and most of them never do it and regret it after their parents die."

It was true. After that talk with my mom, I felt a huge weight lifted off my shoulders. I was surprised, because I didn't even know I was carrying all of that.

It was one more thing that Dan was doing for me. He made me examine my life choices and face my most meaningful relationships. All of that work was part of my attempt to clear my channel, so he would eventually be able to conncct, to communicate.

GOING TO SEE THE DOLPHINS

May 2009

Alex and I were finally on the plane to Key West. Our flight to Florida was short and great. We were not even in a hurry to get there. Just knowing we were by ourselves and had nobody to care for was enough to put us at peace. When we got to Miami and took the small plane to Key West, we really started to feel we were on vacation. The view from the windows was breathtaking. Turquoise water as far as the eye could see dotted with white sandy islands with green spots.

We got to the little airport and waited for our shuttle to the hotel. I started browsing through some flyers on the counter. Suddenly something caught my eye. It was a leaflet for a day trip sailing to see dolphins in the wild.

To my surprise, Alex immediately agreed to go. After all, we were on vacation. A few hours of sailing, getting a tan and watching the beautiful creatures would not hurt us. We went there on our third day. By that time we were rested and happy. The first dolphin we saw was a baby one. It was swimming by itself, just behind his family. After a few more minutes of following it, we saw the rest of them too, swimming in pairs and groups. They were beautiful. Alex loved them too.

It was such a thrilling experience, seeing the dolphins swim. I used to dive in the Red Sea when I was younger, and I always loved water and ocean creatures. I loved the feeling of being surrounded by Parrot Fish and Angel Fish, all swimming around me displaying their bright reds, pinks, greens and yellows. It had been years since I've done that. It was the first time I'd done anything close to that with Alex. Experiencing this with the man I loved next to me made it so special.

The beautiful dolphins made me think of Dan. I thought about that baby swimming by itself, beautiful and happy. He knew his family was just a little ways ahead of him. He did not mind. He knew they were there, and he knew he could be with them at any given moment, if he chose to. He just felt like being by himself.

Will you ever choose to join us, Dan?

And surrounded by blue water, being kissed by the wind and the sun, I knew that the answer was yes.

PANIC

June 2009

My friend Michelle called me just as I was coming out of the gym. Michelle has two children with autism.

"Hey!" I said cheerfully as soon as I saw it was her number on the screen.

"Hey..." She was crying.

"What's going on?" I stopped in my tracks.

"I just got out of the PPT."

PPT stands for "planning and placement meeting." This was a meeting at school that takes place once a year to review the child's progress, and create goals and objectives for the coming school year. Usually, all the people involved come: the special education teacher, speech pathologist, occupational therapist, social worker and school psychologist. Anyone involved in the child's school plan is included.

This was an opportunity to hear about how our kids were doing, but autism parents usually dread the PPT. Sometimes our kids were not doing well and having a hard time. Even when our kids *were* doing well, looking at their goals and objectives on the Individualized Educational Plan (IEP) made us want to cry. At age 8 the goal for math could be "count to 10." You often felt like your child was not moving fast enough. It showed, yet again, how far your child was from being "typical."

When I heard Michelle's voice, I could imagine two things that might have gone wrong: one is that her town did not approve sending her children to Good School for another year, which would mean complete disaster; or two, that she was not happy with how her kids were progressing. I was hoping that it was the second, which was the more common disappointment.

"Where are you?"

"Still in the school parking lot."

"Meet me at our place. I will be there in twenty minutes."

"OK," I heard her sniffing.

Shortly after that we were sitting across from each other in our favorite diner. We were both quiet.

After a few sips of coffee Michelle finally lifted her eyes from her cup. I could see the puffiness under her eyes.

I smiled. She smiled back at me but her eyes remained teary.

"We got one more year."

"Wow, that's great!"

Alex and I were still paying for the school and being obsessed with getting the district to pay made me feel that if I had that covered, I would be the happiest person on the planet. I knew this had been Michelle's big fear before the meeting, that her district would discontinue the outplacement. But then she got what she wanted. What else could have gone wrong?

"Yes. That part *is* great."

"Who was at the PPT?" I asked, thinking that if we had a conversation we would eventually get to the part that was bothering her so much. I was also hoping that there were more good things. I wanted to hear about those.

"Vicky, Rachel, Karen," Michelle mentioned the names of all the teachers we both loved.

"Myra?" I asked. Lady Einstein, our beloved director was always there when those meetings took place. She was always making sure our kids were taken care of, and that we, the parents, understood everything and that our concerns were addressed.

"Yes," Michelle smiled, to show me that Myra was not the problem.

I waited.

"Kara was there too."

Kara was the head speech pathologist. She was brilliant. I remembered her from the first day

Alex and I came to see the school. Dan really liked her and I did too.

"Leo is doing fine. At a snail's pace but getting there. Lily is the problem. Kara was going over the speech goals and they stayed exactly the same as last year. I asked her what was going on and she said she was not sure. They are still stuck on requesting."

See the way it goes is they teach our kids to request first, then to answer questions, then to tell things that have happened, and eventually we all pray that they will be able to hold a conversation. It is very difficult to know in the early stages.

Our kids did get stuck. The thing is, if your child is at the best school with the best experts in speech therapy, and that still happens, what are you supposed to do?

"Then I asked her if she thought Lily would ever be conversational." Michelle started to cry again.

"And what did she say?"

"She said she does not think so."

Oh no. That didn't make sense. I didn't know why Michelle asked that in the first place. But that answer from Kara did not make sense to me either. They were always so positive at the school.

"What did Myra say?"

Michelle finally smiled. Myra was always positive. That's why all the moms loved her so much. Even when things were bad she always found something positive to say. And in the many years she's been doing this, she had taken those kids a very long way. We knew that and we all trusted her abilities and her opinion.

"Well, you know her. She immediately intervened and said that nothing is set in stone and that there is still time. But she is always so positive, and I am scared that sometimes she is just trying to make me feel better."

"Listen, Lily is a beautiful girl and a wonderful person. You see her. I see her. We know how wonderful she is. She is still little and has time to learn more skills."

Michelle's face lit up a bit.

I reached for her hand.

"She is going to be fine, even if she is not 'conversational' like you and me. She will find a way to communicate with the people she loves. She will have a full and happy life. That is all that matters."

Michelle squeezed my hand back.

"I know. I just want the whole thing. I want the happy ending, you know? I want a miracle."

"Me too," I took a big breath. "Me too."

A few days after that it was my turn to Panic.

I met Alison, another autism mom, in the waiting room of Dan's occupational therapist. Her son was inside with another therapist. We were both waiting. She looked so sad when we walked in, and as soon as Sydney took Dan inside, she started to cry.

"Are you OK?" I asked softly, and she started telling me what had happened. When you are an autism mom taking your child to therapy, chances are you will meet other moms. Many times someone is crying. Sometimes it is you. It makes sense. Our lives are hard. There is always something.

I was willing to support Alison with whatever it was she was facing. We were all facing similar things. But Alison's story surprised and terrified me.

"I have been in bed now for two weeks. I could not take Ben to school. Nothing," she started.

Depression, I thought.

"I could not forgive myself for what happened."

I waited. Sometimes people get into a very rough spot personally or emotionally, but reality is not so bad.

"I could not even leave the bed to take care of him."

"What happened?" I asked.

"He came from school two weeks ago and was not his usual self. He threw his backpack with anger and would not even look at me," she said.

"I noticed that there was something smeared on his glasses and when I touched them and then licked my finger, it was salty. I knew he had been crying a lot. I had never seen him angry like that before. He started throwing things in his room, and then he crawled into his bed and continued to cry for hours.

"He is non-verbal, you know, so I could not understand what happened. All I knew was it was bad."

After a few hours, when evening came and Ben calmed down a bit, she took him to have his bath. That was when she noticed stains on his clothes, and when she tried to wash him he protested and then she saw a bruise: a big, red, swollen bruise on his bottom.

"I was horrified. I got him dressed and rushed to the emergency room. Lucky for me he came with me without too much trouble. The doctor came to see me, after he examined him, and told me that he had called a specialist from the sexual abuse department and she was on her way.

“My boy had been brutally abused that day at school. They could not tell what had been used to penetrate his body, whether it was a pencil or a body part, but his body was injured in a way that indicated beyond doubt that he had been sexually abused using force.”

She looked at me with tears in her eyes.

“How could I have let that happen to him?”

Thunder. Hail. Trees crashing. Hands reaching. Soundless screaming. Glass shatters. Your child being hurt by others is one of the biggest fears of any parent. But children with special needs are so much more helpless.

I felt like I had to do something to help her. She had to take care of her boy. He needed someone to hug him and tell him it will all get better from now on. And the person to do that was his mother. I had to be there for her. I also felt like I had to be there for him.

So I searched inside of me for strength. A tiny, floating light appeared. I held onto it until it got bigger. I looked deep into her teary eyes and told her she is not alone and it is not her fault. I told her that she needed to reach into the part of her that would give her the strength to go on and be with her son. I gave her a long hug and while I was doing it I prayed, "Please give this woman strength. She needs it for her beautiful little boy."

CANCELLING A TRIP

June 2009

Two weeks after that, Alex was supposed to go to Europe for five days for work. It was a trip for a conference that he had booked months before.

A few days before he was supposed to go, I panicked. I found myself with no plan for help. Dara, our babysitter, had already gone home for the summer and so all the other students who could potentially help me.

I was nervous staying home with just the two kids, because Dan had been having behaviors again. Whining, running around and climbing on furniture. I had to be with him every minute of the day just to keep him safe. Gali was still a baby and needed someone with her most of the time.

On the days they had school, I could not see myself accomplishing the task of walking Gali to daycare. What if Dan ran towards the busy street and I could not chase him because I would have Gali with me too? What if when I got her into her "baby room" Dan ran into one of the other rooms and went wild? It is hard to understand until you see it, but kids on the spectrum are very impulsive and so unpredictable. I was scared of the nights. I also knew I could not take them anywhere during the weekend. Two long days of staying home by myself scared the hell out of me. You see, having a child on the spectrum is like having a child who never learned the rules about safety. That is why we constantly needed the ratio of one to one with the kids, even when Dan was almost five. We did not know what he could be doing while unattended. He could go to the stove and turn it on. He could climb on the counter and break a glass, and we would not even know. All those thoughts were running through my head. I could not possibly see myself doing it.

The problem was that the trip was really important to Alex. Not only was he supposed to participate in a conference that he really wanted to be in, he was also supposed to meet one of his best friends from Israel who was also attending.

I felt completely torn. I did not know what scared me more, staying with both kids by myself, or telling Alex that I wanted him to cancel the trip he was so looking forward to.

The day before he was supposed to go, I broke down in tears.

“Do you want me to cancel?” Alex asked me quietly.

“I think I do,” I whispered. “Do you think you can do that?”

He did. He called everyone and explained that his son who had autism was having a hard time. As much as I felt terrible about ruining his trip, I was also happy. I was proud of Alex. I felt good about what an amazing husband and dad he was. And it was also the first time he used those words with people. He called the person who arranged the conference and the airline and his friend the professor and told all of them about Dan.

As the years go by, and we are still faced with Dan’s challenges, I get to see how deep Alex’s love is for him. Thanks to Dan, his fatherhood is deep and immense. He is the best dad to all of his children, yet when I watch him find the mental powers to help Dan with such kindness and love, my heart fills with joy and I feel very lucky. I also know that I would never have seen this side of him if it wasn't for Dan.

MY STEPCHILDREN

June 2009

One morning my fifteen year old stepson Tomer called Alex with big news. He told Alex that his mom agreed to let him come and live with us in the U.S. Tomer had been talking about moving to live with his dad for a long time. It was always the same discussion where Alex and I told him that we would be delighted to have him, as long as his mom was OK with it. She never was. Until now.

I was very excited to hear the news. Even though they lived so far from us, Shira and Tomer were a big part of not only Alex's life, but also mine, Dan and Gali's.

***

The first time they came to visit Alex and me was when we lived together in New York. It was before Dan was born. Alex and I lived in a beautiful two-bedroom apartment on the Upper West Side in Manhattan. We spent our time after work going out to restaurants, seeing friends, and enjoying the park on weekends. We had a wonderful routine. Our apartment was neat and we loved having people over and cooking dinners, or just ordering in and watching TV.

When the kids were about to arrive for a visit, I could not stop thinking about the day I saw them eating popsicles on the couch in front of the TV at Alex's apartment in Israel. The popsicles dripped over the couch and rug. I could not imagine what would happen when they arrived at our apartment.

I talked about it with a friend from work. I was working at a law firm at the time. My friend noticed I was nervous about the visit, and he was determined to help me figure it out. After brainstorming about it, I realized that if I made four simple rules, I could control the situation and make sure the apartment stayed the same. Rule number one, no eating anywhere in the apartment except at the table. Rule number two, shoes off before entering. Rule number three, no putting feet onto any furniture. Rule number four, hands washed when coming home.

You can probably tell I was not comfortable and not ready for the big change a child in your life really means. I was comfortable setting boundaries with them just like with my soldiers. Years later I realized how hard it is for me to set rules and create boundaries for my own kids.

According to the schedule Alex had with his ex-wife, the kids were supposed to come visit shortly after Dan was born. He was two months old when they arrived. As much as I liked having them around, I could not imagine them coming at this particular time. I was exhausted. Alex was working. I was supposed to take care of Dan while entertaining the big kids somehow during the long hours he was at work. All I wanted was to be with Dan and sleep when he was taking naps.

The kids were supposed to stay in the second bedroom, the room Dan was supposed to move into when he turned three months. We already had his crib and his toys there. I did not want the kids messing any of it up. 'Maybe we will have them sleep in the living room?' I thought.

My friend Sheila came to visit me the day before they arrived. She had a two-year-old boy. I did not see her often because she lived in New Jersey but she would sometimes join the big

Israeli group we belonged to. I told her that I did not know what to do about the kids' visit and how I did not want them messing with Dan's things. She stopped playing with Dan and looked at me in complete disbelief. "Are you completely insane?" she said. "Don't want them messing with his things? How are they going to feel? And also, just so you know, babies *love* big kids. You have to see them as a good addition to Dan's life and not as interference."

I decided to follow her advice.

The kids' visit turned out to be a wonderful experience. We had the best time. It was very different from my regular routine but I found myself enjoying it. One day we decided to surprise Alex and meet him for lunch at Patsy's Pizza, which was close to the law school. I bundled Dan up and the kids and I hopped into a cab to head downtown. There was snow everywhere and we squeezed in the backseat of the cab, next to Dan's carseat. We watched the people walking outside in the freezing breeze, while we were warming up inside the car, and played games all the way to the pizza place. Each one of us had to choose a word, and then the others had to find a song that had the word in it. Whoever found a song first, got to say the next word and have the other two find songs, and so on.

One evening when we were all having dinner, Dan stayed up with us. It was not a time he was usually awake. I placed him in the bassinet next to the dinner table so we could eat and he was waving his feet and hands in the air happily. Suddenly I heard him laugh aloud. Tomer, who was sitting across from me at the table, and next to the bassinet, looked at me surprised. He heard it too.

Dan started laughing when he was only two months old at the same time that Tomer and Shira were visiting. I started to see Tomer and Shira in a completely different light after that. They were the kids that made Dan happy and I was going to do everything in my power to make them happy too.

The thing about the visit was that Tomer did not want to go back. He hid behind the sofa when it was time to leave for the airport and cried his heart out when it was time to say goodbye.

Besides the difficulty of saying goodbye, we always had a great time when Tomer and Shira came to visit. When Dan started crawling, they would crawl with him around the apartment. When Dan was big enough to walk, they played ball with him in the park. When Dan was almost two, Tomer taught him how to throw acorns in the air. They would make fun songs about Dan. Every time they came we would all have a boost of positive energy.

***

And a few years later there we were, hearing Tomer's news.

There were so many things to be done before he could move and start a new life with us. The biggest task was finding a new place for our family.

I remembered how traumatic our move from New York to Connecticut was for Dan and it scared me at first. But then I remembered that everything else would stay the same for him. School, friends, town, and that would probably make it easier. I kept telling myself that he was much older at this point and understood so much more.

I was still digesting the fact that we would have a teenager living with us. Some parts of it were scary: what if he did not behave the way he did while he was visiting? After all, when he was coming to visit he was only spending time with us. Now he would have his own life too. He would have schoolwork, and college was just around the corner.

But then I started seeing the other possibilities: having another person who is almost a grown up and very reliable, meant we would be more free. We would not have to worry about both of us being home when the kids were not at school. We could even go to the store by ourselves if we needed something, because there would be another pair of helping hands. And in general, especially if we lived in a house, one of us could go rest in the bedroom while both kids are home. Between the three of us, there were so many more possibilities.

And then another thought came to my mind. What if I went to Israel for a visit? I hadn't been there in three and a half years, since that traumatic visit when Dan got sick. What if I took Gali and got on a plane to visit my family? My sisters had not even seen her yet. She was two and I knew I would have the best time with her. And since Tomer would be there with Alex and Dan's time was completely booked with summer day camp, they would be fine.

JOSEPH'S ASSIGNMETS

June 2009

When I spoke to Joseph that week and told him about my idea to visit Israel, he was very excited.

"Yes, come! We will do some spiritual work. You will get to spend time with Gali, which means you will be creating positive energy around Dan."

"What?" I asked, puzzled.

"Yes, when you are doing something you are enjoying you are creating positive energy. That means the spirits have less room to come close and bother Dan. Being alone with Gali and seeing your family and friends will help you create more positive energy. And it is a good idea for Dan to spend time with Alex. And we can do some work!"

When I asked him what exactly he was thinking, it turned out that Joseph's idea of work was to take me to visit holy graves in the northern part of Israel, to meet with Kabala people and to cleanse myself from negative energy.

'I could do that,' I thought. It was not exactly my idea of fun. I wanted to go to the beach and enjoy the clear water and warm sun. I wanted to go to my favorite restaurant, sit at a table under the white umbrella, eat the delicious seafood and fresh salads and drink white wine. I wanted to see as many friends as I could and spend quality time with my family. But I could squeeze some spiritual work in, especially if it would help Dan.

The funny thing about Joseph was that sometimes his idea of spiritual work *was* my ideas of fun. As part of going through a "forgiveness process," Joseph suggested that I go to my favorite coffee shop and write a list of all the people I had issues with and create a "forgiveness list." No matter how old the issues were nor what age I was when the incidents occurred. Any person who makes me feel negative was supposed to be on that list. "If you are not sure, notice how your body feels when you think of certain people. If any part of your body tightens when you are thinking about them, even just a little, they should be on the forgiveness list," he said. Joseph believed that once I managed to forgive the people on the list, I would "clear my channel" and make room for positive things.

"Having negative thoughts about people who made you feel bad in the past hurts only you. It is a waste of space that you could be using for positive energy. Let it go and you will feel much better. Just like after that talk with your mother, remember?"

I remembered. So I went to my favorite coffee shop and worked on that.

Joseph once told me to go to the mall to observe people; He told me to get myself new shoes; He encouraged me to continue with my zumba; He told me to cook and bake when he felt I needed grounding.

The 'work' he made me do was often fun.

But joining him for a whole day in Israel's August heat to see holy places, caves and tombs? Well, anything for Dan.

I still needed to think about whether I would be able to pull off the trip. There was a house to find before I did that. There was the meeting with our town to attend. And there was only one me.

"We'll see," was all he got from me at the end of the conversation.

MEETING WITH THE TOWN

July 2009

At the same time we were conducting the independent evaluations for Dan, we contacted our town in order to request a program.

As much as I knew this was something that I had to do, it was not easy. When I came in for the initial meeting with the district, I met a team of people who were very sweet and really wanted to help. Everyone was so nice. They listened to what I had to say and informed me of their plan to test Dan. I felt horrible. Here were a group of people hoping to help Dan and wanting to put all their effort into it, and all I wanted was to reject the program they offered, and place Dan at Good School anyway.

I had to work very hard on separating our plan from the people I was meeting with. It was Dan's life we were talking about, I thought. I had to play the game. I decided to not think about it until our big meeting scheduled for the summer.

For some weird reason it was scheduled on my birthday! Did that mean I was going to get a gift in the form of tuition? That would be the best – and biggest – gift ever.

The meeting day arrived.

The PPT was supposed to include all the experts from the district, the director of special education, and us. The lawyer suggested that she come, as well as Dr. Berger, the psychologist who evaluated Dan, to support our case. She said it would help us understand all the special education terms included in Dan's education plan. I was not sure this was the right thing to do, but it was going to get ugly at some point, so why not now. Maybe this way it would be over faster. But then the school district brought their lawyer too.

We came to the meeting and it was a room full of people. There was so much tension in the air. I hated it.

At the meeting we were in for a complete surprise. Our lawyer had predicted they would come up with a really poor program, one that would make it easy for us to refuse. Then we could move forward and demand the placement at Good School. But the district surprised us - and our attorney - and came up with a great program.

Of course we knew that Good School was still better for Dan, but what they suggested was good, at least on paper.

There were still things they could not supply. They were not able to deal with Apraxia. That condition, which is a motor system challenge, required specific methods that they were not familiar with. Good School had expert therapists for that. They could also not provide the sensory environment that Dan needed. The special needs classroom was very small and busy. I knew Dan's sensory system would not be able to handle it.

So we said no.

I felt terrible because I realized how hard they had worked to try and make something work for Dan. As our lawyer and I continued the conversation privately, still in the building because it was raining outside, she convinced me we were doing the right thing, because even if they did what they promised, the program would never be as good as the one at Good School.

We were about to leave the building when I realized I had forgotten my umbrella in the meeting room.

I went back announcing myself by knocking loudly on the door. I did not want them to think I wanted to eavesdrop. As I stepped in, I saw everyone standing around the table, except the special education director who was still sitting. The school's lawyer stood there with a big smile on her face. She just got another case to litigate, to make more money. The speech pathologist and school psychologist and all the other advisors from the different departments were surrounding the director, who looked devastated. I suddenly realized this was clearly a personal disappointment for her.

She had worked so hard to come up with this program. She really had. She thought they had come up with something good. And we threw it all back in her face. I felt bad. I felt that something was not right. It was as though this was a show being performed for me, but not done on my terms.

I suddenly remembered the conversation I had with Teresa a few weeks earlier. I called her to talk about a dream I had.

"Do you have trouble with money these days?" she asked me. I explained to her our biggest money issue right then was getting money for tuition.

"But you are doing it all wrong!" she said. "You will not get it through fighting. You need to go with good intentions. Did I not teach you anything? Use your skills to find out what the other side feels. You need to listen."

When I saw those people in the meeting room, I understood. I saw her, the director. I felt her. And her facial expression was the most powerful and most important thing I took from that meeting. That and the school's lawyer smiling. It all came together for me.

Another sad thing about it was that if we went ahead and sued the school district, the representation for litigation in court was going to cost us anywhere from $30,000 to $80,000. We didn't have that kind of money. And it didn't make sense to do it, because the program they offered was good. It was the lawyer and the psychologist who said their experience showed that public schools do not follow through. And that even if they did, it would never be the same quality as Dan was already getting. But in a court, we would probably lose.

The next few days were a blur. I had no clue what we were going to do. It was clear that the district was not going to pay for Dan's tuition at Good School, and I was afraid of what another transition would do to Dan.

He was doing so well at Good School. It was the first time we were sure that the program he was attending was the best for him. It gave us so much peace. And it was the first time I could do things for myself: I could meet the moms and I did not have to be on the clock and run and pick Dan up early and drive him to therapy in the middle of the day.

And most importantly: he was doing well constantly. No ups and downs, no great beginning and then disappointment. How could I ever be sure that this would happen at another school? We had already had so many disappointments.

I called Myra the director of Good School to tell her about the PPT. I thought maybe she could help in some way. Maybe they had a secret scholarship for parents who failed completely because the district gave them too good a program on paper and so they have no chance in court. A scholarship for those who really tried and did everything they could. I told her we were offered a good program. I also told her it would not make sense to pay for a lawyer and sue them in court. And then it came to me.

What if I did it myself? I am a lawyer.

Myra thought it was a great idea. She said she would help me. She would prepare me with all the professional knowledge I needed about special education. I figured Alex would do the legal research. And I would coordinate it all into a beautiful court appearance that would get us the money we needed!

Interesting how life takes you places. I always felt like Dan's challenges took me away from practicing law, and drove me towards natural healing and then writing. Well, maybe not. It seemed I was being forced to take some steps in the legal direction again.

Then I remembered the feeling I had at the meeting. The feeling that this was a big show. One that was created for me that I was starring in, but did not like at all. I don't like conflicts. There had to be another way.

I decided I should call Laura, the special education director, from the meeting. I remembered how they were all surrounding her, and how nobody was happy but the lawyer. I knew she did not like this show either. I did not know what this would bring, but something told me it was the right thing to do.

First, I thanked her. I told her that I could see how hard she had worked to create the program for Dan. I told her how much I appreciated it. I said I had decided to tell her that, as a mother to an educator, without all the show with the lawyers around. I told her it was thoughtful and that the program could have been great, if Dan did not have the additional challenge of apraxia. I also told her that even though I was a lawyer, I changed direction to healing because I don't like to battle, and that I think two people can reach an agreement without spending money on lawyers and without taking a long path of conflict. I told her I didn't want to fight and I wanted to find a way for our family and the district to be happy.

She thanked me. I could hear in her voice how much she appreciated that. I had a feeling she would help me. She said that she was not the decision maker, but that she would talk to her supervisor and get back to me. She also didn't believe a battle was a good idea, and that a compromise is always better.

I called our lawyer to tell her we weren't going ahead with the lawsuit, because I was planning to sit down and talk to the people from the district first to see if maybe we could resolve this on our own. The lawyer was very skeptical. "Good luck to you Shirley, but if those people give you a dime after this meeting, I will eat my shirt," she said.

PREPARATION FOR THE TRIP

August 2009

It was decided. Gali and I would go to Israel to visit the family, while Alex and Tomer stayed with Dan. Tomer arrived at the beginning of August and we had one week to spend together before Gali and I went to Israel.

When Tomer first arrived, it felt like all the other times he came to visit. The only difference was that he brought one extra suitcase and that he was more nervous than usual. Yet he hid it well so we did not know how nervous he was and how hard it had been for him to leave everyone back home and come here.

During that week we had together until the trip, I took him to see the new house that I had managed to find for our family. It was a huge, very old house in the same town. We could have looked in neighboring towns, but since we had already established a relationship with our district regarding schooling for Dan, I did not want to move to another town and start the process over.

There was not a large selection of houses and there was not much time, so we signed a contract with a very nice older guy to rent his beautiful old house in a nice neighborhood in our town. The plan was to move the first week of September.

I scheduled the move with a moving company and then focused my attention on getting ready for the trip to see the family. It had been four years since I visited last, at that miserable time when Dan got sick.

Funnily enough most of the preparations turned out to be instructing Alex and Tomer for the stay with Dan. I had to make sure they had everything they needed in order to follow the strict diet Dan was on at the time: sugar-free, gluten-free and casein-free. He loved coconut popsicles that I made for him. I would sweeten those with Stevia, a natural sweetener that our very strict doctor approved. I had to make sure I made enough of those.

I also needed to make sure they had the right breads and baked goods. Tomer volunteered to join me on a trip - an hour ride each way – to a specialized bakery that sold fresh gluten-free, sugar-free goods.

The last thing I did before the ride to the airport arrived, was bake my special almond-flour-bread that I knew Dan liked. Tomer liked that one too and it worked well for him since he was on a no-carbs diet at the time. I was happy Tomer was on that diet. For one, he looked better than ever, which was great because he was sixteen and about to start a new life in a new place. Also, his diet matched Dan's diet perfectly because they both needed high protein intake, which meant I could trust him to tell Alex what Dan could and could not have in my absence.

When the airport ride arrived, the bread was still in the oven. Tomer promised me to get it out on time.

I left the house with Gali, certain that the boys had it all under control. I then allowed myself to get excited about the trip. I was also a bit nervous about the day-of-work that Joseph had planned for me.

MY DAD

My dad was the one who volunteered to accompany me on my trip to meet Joseph and "do spiritual work." It was part of my dad's belief that we need to do everything and anything we can to help Dan.

After Dan was diagnosed with autism, I had a really difficult time with my dad. He kept insisting that there was nothing wrong with Dan and that he only had "defiance of authority issues."

When Alex and I were going through all the evaluations and I started reading about autism and slowly stepping out of my denial, my dad was arguing with me constantly. He kept on suggesting ways to handle Dan and his challenges.

"Shirley," he said on the phone, "if only you taught him how to behave, he would not be like that. You need to teach him how to sit when you tell him and follow you when you are out of the house. Just like that time in the park when we visited you in New York..."

"The park?"

"Yes, he was running and it was dangerous, and you did not stop him!"

My dad was referring to a particularly miserable Easter Sunday in Central Park when he and my mom came to visit. Dan was two and we had no idea why he was doing certain things. That day the park was filled with so many people, and Dan was so overwhelmed with the noise that he bolted out of his stroller and just ran and ran. I could barely get hold of him. I had to hold his squirming body in my arms and carry him all the way home. Luckily Dan was still small enough for that to be possible.

My dad mentioning this occasion made me explode. I understood that he was in denial and that he was blaming me for Dan's situation. What he said sounded to me like "if only you were a better mother and you disciplined Dan, things would be better."

"Call me when you are ready to have a knowledgeable conversation and not question me with no basis," I said and hung up. I then emailed him a list of books that I had already read.

Months later my mom told me he felt so guilty that night that he did not sleep at all. After that he started learning more about autism, which made him an equal partner in discussions about Dan and his progress, which was a huge relief. Autism is like a language. You cannot talk about all of its complexities with someone who does not understand.

After my dad learned more, he would come up with good suggestions. It was thanks to him that I started teaching Dan math – "He can be an engineer, you'll see!" – and got a basketball hoop to play with Dan outside. Later he was the one who suggested teaching Dan how to type.

If you ever hear of a basketball player or a Nobel Prize winner named Dan Stein, know that he got there in great part thanks to his grandpa.

TRIP TO ISRAEL

August 2009

I was very thankful to my dad for volunteering to come with me and drive Joseph and me everywhere we needed to go. Joseph lived two hours driving distance from my parents' house and the driving between all the holy places was going to be long as well. Not to mention the two hours drive back home after we dropped Joseph off.

The night before the trip I spoke to Joseph and we made final plans. He told me how to find our meeting point, a crossroad in the middle of nowhere. I asked him if he felt safe leaving his car there for the whole day. "I will take a taxi there, I cannot drive, Shirley," he said to me. I was wondering about that. I had this fantasy that he would be living just like any other person. I started to realize it was not exactly true.

The next morning, when my dad and I arrived at the meeting point, which looked like the middle of nowhere, just roads and sand surrounding us, I got out of the car to greet Joseph. He was a big guy with short black curly hair and brown eyes. He was wearing jeans and a white buttoned shirt. He looked completely normal to me. We hugged and I felt confused and disoriented for a minute. Here I was meeting in person the man I got so used to talking to on the phone. We spoke every week and by now he knew so much about me. Suddenly, I felt exposed.

My dad was the one who came to my rescue at this point. He came out of the car and shook Joseph's hand, and when we started to drive he began a conversation. He was very curious to hear Joseph's story directly from him.

My dad's attitude towards this trip was very practical: it doesn't matter what we say or do today. We are doing this to help Dan, and whatever comes out of it is great. If nothing happened, at least we know we tried our hardest.

The first stop on our trip was a grocery store. I had no idea what this was about, but I followed Joseph inside. Joseph gave me an assignment: to walk around and try to feel what I was receiving from the people around me. Just a few steps into the store, I was overcome by the wonderful smell of fresh baked goods from the bakery.

Then we passed by the refrigerator and I saw all my favorite dairy products. This assignment which seemed so simple at first turned out to be so hard. I had been missing the food from home so much. I grabbed a cart and started picking up some of my favorite things.

When I looked up and saw Joseph's face I knew I had done something wrong.

"You should concentrate on the assignment. Actually, since we are going to be doing so much spiritual work, you should not eat anything, only drink."

I was not prepared for that at all. I had barely eaten anything before my dad and I left the house, at 6 am, and now I was supposed to go on like that all day? But there was nothing I would not do to make this experience successful, so I ignored my cravings and put the cart away.

After the grocery store we stopped at a mall. Joseph said he was going to teach me about the spirits. We went to a movie theater on the top floor. They had very large figures of actors and characters. They looked like huge statues. "Shirley," Joseph said, "This is what they look like for Dan."

We both stood close to the statues and they felt so big. I remembered how Dan was attracted to statues in Central Park and how he was obsessed with this one figure of a man at our JCC. Now it all started to make sense to me. I was starting to comprehend how it must have felt for Dan to be surrounded by such sights all the time. I mean, if I was to take Joseph's word, things like that were surrounding Dan all the time. He was paying more attention to them than to the real people around him. Now I could see why he was so distracted.

We stopped for coffee. I got permission to drink a smoothie. The sweetness of the strawberries and dates combined with the coolness of the cold milk and crushed ice were so refreshing. That was supposed to keep me going for the long day we had ahead of us. When we sat down my dad told Joseph that he couldn't see any trace of autism in him. "What an amazing recovery."

The thing was *I* could. I could see that Joseph's eye contact was slightly off. I could see him moving more than a regular person. When he was standing up he moved his weight from one foot to the other. When he was sitting he would fidget. It was like the stimming Dan did, only milder. He wasn't flapping his arms yet he still needed movement. I kept reimagining our talks and how deep and wise his thoughts and directions have always been. And here he was, still demonstrating autism traits. I needed to work hard on putting together the image I had in my head and what I was seeing in front of me.

After the coffee break, we drove for a long time and stopped at our first holy grave. The grave was inside an old cave. It was small with low ceilings. There were lots of prayer books placed on tables along the walls. The odor was that of an old place. Moldy and dusty. I went in through the women's separate passage. All the Jewish holy places include a separation between women and men. When I came out of my side to look for Joseph and my dad, a young rabbi approached me. He was collecting money for his Yeshiva. I gave him some. "Tell me why you are here, and we will pray for you," he said.

"I am here for my son, Dan."

"And what do you want us to pray for?"

I paused for a minute. My heart was beating fast. How do I define my wish? Do I want God to take Dan's autism away? I had to be specific. He needed to write something down. What *did* I want?

"Pray for Dan to join us, his family. To communicate with us."

I saw Joseph and my dad coming out and I joined them.

From there, we were supposed to drive for a while up the mountain to a site I had never heard of. Even though we were in Israel, I had never explored this part of the country. Since my dad was the one driving and Joseph was the one planning, I decided to not be involved in the actual facts of where we are and dedicate myself solely to the spiritual part of it.

I was already exhausted by this time, so I tried to sleep in the car. I was sitting in the back and Joseph was sitting in the front with my dad. The road up the mountain was steep and my dad kept trying to wake me up. I knew what he was thinking: if something happened to the car he wanted me to be alert. But I was tired! "I'm up, I'm up," I mumbled every time he tried to wake me, and then I would continue to sleep. Before we arrived at our next destination, Joseph asked my dad to stop the car and asked me to take a walk with him. It was still early in the day, but it was so hot already. We walked among the old dusty Acacia trees and Joseph asked me why I was responding to my father's requests that way.

"Because I am tired! And nothing will happen to the car anyway. He is such a cautious driver."

"So tell him what you want. Be direct. Stop apologizing."

We walked back to the car and Joseph gave my dad directions to our next stop. It was a small cave surrounded with a yard and fenced in. We were in the middle of nowhere. When we walked towards it, I could see the Sea of Galilee. The ancient country lay below us. Majestic and silent mountains surrounded the blue eye, the Sea. I stopped breathing for a moment before that heavenly sight.

Joseph had me sit down on a boulder and sat next to me.

"I want to teach you how to spot the spirits. Look at that tree," he said. "Can you see the top?" I nodded. "Now concentrate. Look at what is just above the top."

I looked and concentrated, and then I saw it. It was like a cloud on top of it. It was white, almost clear, but I could definitely see it.

"Now look there. Can you see it on top of that tree?"

I concentrated and then nodded again.

"Now you can see it. It will help you, because they are everywhere. At least you will be able to tell when they are present. Dan still experiences it differently, but at least you will know they are there."

We went back to the car and my dad drove for a while. Then Joseph asked him to stop and he asked me to go sit with him on a bench on the side of the road. By that time, we were much closer to the Sea of Galilee. I could see the line where the deep blue water met the clear blue sky. It was very quiet there. All we could hear was the chirping of the birds and the leaves moving in the light breeze.

"Close your eyes," Joseph asked me. He waited a few seconds before he continued, softly: "Notice how you are feeling right now. How does your body feel. How do you feel inside." He paused again, and then asked: “You are peaceful and relaxed, right?”

I nodded.

“Now picture Dan.”

I did. I pictured Dan’s beautiful face. When he appeared before my eyes I immediately felt a knot in my stomach. What was that? Fear? Definitely stress.

“I want you to connect in your mind the feeling you are experiencing now, with the image of Dan. Can you do that?”

I realized that Joseph was trying to cut the connection that I had for so long of being stressed when I thought of Dan. I was scared when I thought about him, too. Joseph wanted to replace those negative feelings with peace and calmness, the way I felt at that moment.

“I understand. I will try to do that more, but it will take real work to succeed.”

"I know," he smiled. "I wanted you to experience it at least once with me, so you would know how to do it at home."

Joseph took me to more and more sites that day. I stopped counting. There was always something he wanted me to say or think about. At one of the places we went to he asked me to enter a little cave. It was round and had a low ceiling. There were remains of many candles there and books that people had left there. "Pick up one of the books, read it. See what it says."

I opened one of the Zohar books that were on the floor. I could not understand most of the ancient language, yet I could recognize the word "love." I stayed in there for a few more minutes. On my way out, when I leaned forward to avoid the very low exit, I felt something "land" on my head. It felt like a hat or a crown, but I knew it was energy. "What was that?" I asked Joseph, "I feel something sitting on my head now."

"Yes," Joseph laughed. "It is a spirit, a positive one. It's OK."

We continued. In between sites I fell asleep. This spiritual stuff was really hard. They did not call it 'spiritual work' for nothing. In between naps,

I could hear my dad talk to Joseph about the bible and Jewish history. My dad was showing off his knowledge of what he thought to be Joseph's interest and Joseph was glad to listen, and learn about my dad himself just as much as he learned about what he was telling him.

I woke up a short while later to see that we had arrived at a very busy place. There were many people walking around and drivers were competing over parking spots in the small, unpaved parking lot.

'Someone important must be buried here,' I thought.

"This is the grave of Rabbi Meyer," Joseph announced. "You are about to meet a very good friend of mine."

Before I could decide whether he was joking and meant the dead rabbi or was referring to a real person, my dad and I followed him to a very large courtyard crowded with people. Women wearing headscarves in all different colors, men in suits and black hats, and families with small children filled the place. Masses of people were making their way in and out of the building at the end of the courtyard. We saw Joseph hug an older man who was standing in front of a small charcoal grill.

"This is Ezra!" Joseph announced proudly, as if we were supposed to know of him. Ezra was surrounded by a large crowd and was performing some ritual that required burning powders. When I got closer I recognized the smell. They were the same powders that Joseph had sent me a few months earlier to cleanse our apartment from negative energy.

As Joseph explained to us about Ezra's special ability to 'perceive things about people,' I could hear Ezra talking to a woman who came to see him with her four children. She was ill. There was a line of people behind her who also came to see Ezra.

While we were standing there waiting for Ezra to prepare our own ceremony, an older woman who was passing by stopped and looked at me with a very serious expression. "This guy is very helpful," she pointed at Ezra. "Take what he gives you and put it in a central spot in your home." I looked and saw that Ezra was making me a certificate. He asked for my name and my mom's name and when I was born and started writing the names of all the angels who were guarding me. Then he took some powders and threw them onto his grill. The smoke filled the air around me.

“You need to face the facts, the real truth. Pray to God and with God’s help things will get better.”

‘What was he saying?’ I thought. ‘I am facing the facts. I am not in denial anymore. I know that if I do everything right I will not even have to deal with autism anymore. I am doing everything right. I am learning. I am healing. I will get there. Dan will get there. It is just a matter of time!’

I turned to Joseph. “Why did he say that to me? Does this mean Dan will not be OK?”

“Don’t worry about that now. We will talk about it later.”

I had to go through one more ceremony with Ezra. He took me to a shed a few steps from his ceremony spot. He was going to perform a ceremony to remove negative energies from me. There was water and a knife and something that exploded in the water and then over my head.

“Wow, so many!” Joseph said, watching from the door. Ezra put some pieces of metal, “the remains of the bad energy," in a bag and Joseph told me we would get rid of those later.

It was time for me to enter the holy grave of Rabi Meyer. It was a small space below the ground. I stepped down carefully. There were many prayer books and candles there. It was a small space and it felt claustrophobic. I stood there and looked at the signs and the notes people left there. Every note had a prayer written on it. I was so exhausted by then. I could not remember what Joseph wanted me to do now. I could not stop thinking about what Ezra had said. Why did he say I had to face the facts? And then trust in God to help.

And then I got it. I remembered what Joseph said to me after I got sunburned a few weeks earlier, about fighting and letting go.

I *was* fighting.

I was fighting this instead of accepting it.

I had to surrender.

Yes, Dan has autism. It is a fact that I need to learn to accept.

And accepting means accepting what it is now. Not accepting it only if he gets better in the future.

Accept it now and that is it.

This is the fighting. And by fighting I am wasting precious energy.

This was the clearing Joseph was talking about. Clearing that out of the way, out of my channel, would enable me to make room for the important stuff, the true healing.

THE VISION

August 2009

There was one more stop on our trip. Joseph said it was a really important part. I could not believe there was more work to do. I was completely exhausted and it was late. It was getting dark. Gali was at my parents' house with my mom. I desperately wanted to see her before she went to bed. But Joseph was not going to give up. I had to finish what he had planned for me.

He instructed my dad to drive to Elijah's cave on Mount Carmel. Elijah was one of the most important prophets in Jewish history. The cave we went to was the place where Elijah stayed when he escaped from the kings of Israel who did not accept his prophecies. There is no grave for Elijah because the story tells that after he was done teaching his apprentice, a carriage with horses made of fire came from the sky and carried him upwards until he disappeared. I later learned that this cave is famous for its healing powers.

When we arrived, Joseph told me to close my eyes. I was going to climb up the steep stairs with my eyes closed. Joseph was going to climb the high stairs with me.

I closed my eyes. Joseph was holding my hand and we started going up. It felt funny to be blinded like that. I also felt lightheaded from fasting all day. I could smell the salty water of the Mediterranean Sea. We were just across from it. I could feel the air change, getting cooler the higher we went. Joseph would warn me if the stairs changed or if we were about to pass an obstacle. During the climb I felt how my senses were sharpened. I didn't feel like my usual self. My body did not matter anymore, just my mind. My thoughts were so clear.

'Does Dan feel this way?' I wondered. 'Did Joseph give me the biggest gift of all, to know how Dan's body feels to him?'

When we entered the area in front of the cave Joseph told me I could open my eyes. I saw his face smiling in front of me.

"Sit here by the tree," he said. Then he asked me if I could see spirits. I looked around me: On the top of the tree; above the streetlight; and on top of the cave entrance. I could not see any. "I cannot see them now, I guess I am too tired," I apologized.

"You are actually OK, there are no spirits here. This place has such pure, positive energy that no negative energy could exist here."

I sighed with relief.

"I want you to go to the end of this area and look down for me," he asked. I did and I saw the Mediterranean Sea dark below us.

"Close your eyes, and see what comes to your mind," he instructed.

I closed my eyes and concentrated. I let my mind finally surrender.

The first thing I saw was green light. And then a face appeared in front of me. It was the face of a woman. Then the face disappeared and the green light turned into a tunnel that looked like a web of green light. At the end of the tunnel I saw an old man with a long beard. I knew this was Elijah. He was coming closer and I could hear his voice talking to me: "As long as you continue to walk the right path and do the right deeds, you will always receive guidance."

And then he disappeared and I saw a vision of the future. It was like someone was playing a recording for me of what would happen in a few years. I saw Dan and Gali. They were still kids, maybe 2 years older than their actual age. Dan looked like himself, only bigger. Gali had really long hair. I saw Dan and me in the kitchen and he was talking to me. There was talk about hot chocolate and a promise that as soon as he finished his homework he would get some. I think he did his homework or brought it for me to see. And then he got some hot chocolate. Then Gali walked in and wanted some too. It was wintertime and we were warm and cozy inside our house. The best part about this picture was that all of us were calm and happy. And that Dan was communicating with me.

Was I making that scene up? I never made the kids hot chocolate and Dan never received homework from school at that time. I was not sure if these were perhaps my secret dreams coming alive before my eyes. I knew this: I was in Elijah's cave and Joseph told me to close my eyes because there was something I needed to see. And this was what I saw. I embraced the moment and was praying deeply that it would come true.

GETTING INTO DAN'S HEAD

September 2009

The week before we moved to the new house, I attended my first autism seminar. The speaker was Raun Kaufman, a charming guy who was severely autistic as a child and was treated with a new method that his parents came up with. After he was healed, his mother opened a center called The Son Rise Program that taught parents and teachers about the method she came up with.

I was interested in hearing about the method because when I read about it on the website, I could tell the principles they based their method on and the techniques they were using were similar to the ones Joseph had been teaching me. Just like Joseph, they believed in joining the child in whatever he was doing, and using those activities to get closer to the child and eventually teach him how to communicate.

This kind of thinking was very different from the “mainstream” methods, such as Applied Behavior Analysis - or ABA, which is the only method that has been scientifically proven to decrease the symptoms and improve the condition of individuals with autism. The mainstream methods focus on discouraging “bad” behaviors or stimming (those behaviors that our kids engage in as a result of their brain’s needs, such as hand flapping, spinning around, etc.)

At the lecture, Raun was talking about how he moved from being severely autistic, not talking or making eye contact at all, to being a completely typical boy. You could honestly not see any traces of autism in him. And to think that when he was two years old the doctors told his parents that he would likely spend his life in an institution.

After the presentation was done I waited to talk to him. I wanted to know more about his personal experience and his perception of autism. I had to know how it truly felt to be inside that bubble. I told him about the things I’ve learned from Joseph and how I practiced those with Dan.

"This is great!" he looked at me with his deep brown eyes and smiled. "It sounds so much like what we do at Son Rise."

He was so genuine and kind that I decided to ask him the main question on my mind. "Do you remember what you were seeing when you still had autism?" I waited to see if he would describe fairies and rainbows, the way Joseph had.

"I don't remember anything special." He shook his head slowly. And then he quickly said, "Wait, I do remember something! I used to see people's faces looking small and floating in the air like they were in bubbles. Just like if you looked through binoculars the wrong way and saw everything small."

Those poor kids, I thought. What a weird way to experience the world. Who knows what other strange ways their brains are capturing the world around them.

"And what are your first memories?"

"My first memory is seeing my mother's face talking to me and smiling."

I was very glad to have learned more about what Dan might be experiencing and to learn that even in the toughest situations there is hope. This guy was in a severe place and now runs a big corporation. There were reasons to remain optimistic.

NEW HOUSE

September 2009

The week after that seminar, our family moved to a new house. Children with autism are very sensitive to changes in their routine and their environment. No matter how we tried to minimize the shock of moving to a new house for Dan by coming to visit the house before we moved, and talking to him about it, when we actually moved, he was in complete chaos, as if plunged into a different and especially negative universe.

The first few days Dan would not leave the kitchen area. He went in there as soon as he came from school and would stay there, sitting by the table.

We could not get him to be comfortable in any of the other rooms. The sleeping situation was the worst.

When we went to see Sydney, Dan's occupational therapist, that Saturday, she asked me, "How is it going with the new house?"

I broke down in tears.

"What happened?" She was worried. She was used to see me strong and optimistic.

"He is having such a hard time," I managed to mumble. "And I don't know what to do to help him."

"What do you see?"

"During the day he is so uncomfortable. It is like he cannot be in the house. He stays in the kitchen, and then maybe the dining room. Now, after a week, he managed to get to the stairs area downstairs. He spends all his days whining and uncomfortable when we are inside. He is only happy outside."

"Do you see him stop before he manages to move from room to room?"

"Yes!" I looked at her surprised.

"And does he feel the surface of the carpet and then the floor?"

"Yes!"

"Well," she said, "A new house is very challenging for a child like Dan. We always assume that kids will be happy immediately and that they will appreciate having more space, but that's not the case."

"Really?"

"You know how he has a hard time knowing where his body ends? That's why we do the deep pressure a lot. So when he is in a familiar environment his body handles itself safely. And you did not have carpets at all in the apartment, right? All the rooms felt the same to him. For him to learn how to move from room to room in the new house is like you and me attempting to climb Mount Everest. It will take his senses time and he will get it but you need to be patient."

"Aha..." I was starting to get it.

"And the same goes for wallpapers. His eyes will take time to get used to them too. And how does the place smell?"

"Oh it's terrible," I said, laughing. "I cannot stand the odor! I am working so hard on airing it and making it smell good!"

"Well, it's even worse for Dan."

She smiled at me and I knew that someday Dan would be able to enjoy the new house. It was his challenge that made everything so hard for him. I was ready to be patient and help him as much as I could.

SLEEPING

September 2009

Dan has been sleeping with Alex and me since he was two and we moved him from a crib to a bed, which he never got used to. This was the worst sleeping situation possible. We weren't able to stretch our bodies and we needed to be careful not to roll over onto him. Also, the bigger Dan became the less space we had for ourselves, not to mention never having grown-up privacy in our own bed. Dan also had to have one of us in bed with him to help him fall asleep. That's why ever since he turned two, my bedtime has been 8 pm.

One of my plans before we moved to the new house was to get Dan to sleep in his own room. When we were still in the apartment and completely optimistic about the move, I spoke to Myra, the director of Good School, who knew Dan very well, and she suggested that we move Dan to his own bed at the same time we moved to the new house.

However, when we moved to the new house, the sleeping situation only got worse. On the day of the move, when the movers arranged our furniture, I kept the kids out of the house in the backyard. We went into the house only after they left. Although the furniture was in its place, there were still dozens of boxes lying around everywhere. Gali didn't mind so much. She was only two. When she got tired, we gave her a bath in the new bathtub and put her to sleep in her crib. She was completely fine and fell asleep.

Dan, however, was in a totally different mindset. He was extremely uncomfortable all evening. The only two rooms he would go into were the kitchen – the back door, which we used to enter the house led there - and the dining room, which was adjacent to the kitchen. He would not go past that point.

When it got late and we wanted to take Dan upstairs, he screamed in protest. Alex and I managed to carry him upstairs together and take him to the bathroom. Luckily he did not run out of the tub and slip on the floor. When we washed Dan, we did it exactly like we used to do in the apartment, rinsing his body with a cup of water.

After the bath we carried him, still in the towel, to our bed. The same bed he had slept in for the last 3 years was there with the familiar sheets. We used his favorite towel too. We had devoted so much time and thought to the transition. Dan got into our bed and finally, after crying loudly for a while, fell asleep. Alex and I unpacked some more boxes and went to sleep. We were exhausted but we were also optimistic. After all, it was not that bad. It could have been worse.

Two hours later it indeed became worse. Dan woke up suddenly. When he realized he was not in a familiar place, he began screaming. Before we knew it, he ran out of bed and down the stairs in the dark. We followed him but there was nothing we could do to calm him down. He was so disoriented. It was like he could not see us.

Downstairs Dan ran around and bounced on the furniture for a long hour. I followed him and tried to engage him, but he was completely in his own world and would not let me do anything to help him. Only when he was completely exhausted, did he fall asleep on the carpet. I went upstairs quickly to get him a blanket and covered him up.

I sat on the sofa in the fully lit living room. I could not possibly go back to my bed and leave him there. I didn't feel safe in the new house yet. I missed the security of living in an apartment building where you have a doorman and you know you're surrounded by people.

The same scenario repeated for two weeks. Dan would wake up, go downstairs, and run through the house until he collapsed. On one of those nights, it took Dan an especially long time to go back to sleep. But then when he did, I sat there looking at the huge living room. I had wanted to be in a big house so much but now could not even enjoy it. Why did we move here? I cried. After a while I eventually fell asleep on the sofa sitting up.

I suddenly felt someone touching my shoulder. I jumped up ready for the worst. I saw the fully lit living room. The cable box showed 2 am. It was my stepson Tomer, who had come downstairs.

"Go back to bed," he said softly. "I got him."

"No, it's OK,"

"Go."

"But you have school tomorrow."

He simply lay down on the floor next to Dan and covered himself with the blanket.

In spite of the terrorized nights – I thanked God that Gali never woke up - the days were a bit better. After Dan woke up downstairs, we managed to get him ready for school. Then he would come home and play in the kitchen and sometimes in the dining room until evening. When the weather was nice we took advantage of that and went outside to the backyard. Dan was much happier being outside.

I still wanted to move Dan to his own bed.

At last, I decided to complete the first step: setting Dan's room up. I went to the store to get a new bed, one that was similar to the bed Alex and I had. I figured the more familiar the bed, the better. I also got sheets that matched ours.

The next day we put the bed together and got the room ready. I unpacked some more boxes and brought in some of Dan's toys. I set up a new easel I had bought.

That weekend I called everyone to the new room. Gali was excited about another new thing in the house. Within minutes, she and Dan were happily painting on the easel. Alex and Tomer cooperated with me and came to hang out in Dan's new room.

Ten minutes after Dan and Gali went into the room, we had two beautiful paintings. Gali's was made with a brush and Dan's made with his hands. Of course he did not stop with painting on the paper. He painted with his hands all over the easel and also a little bit on the wall. It was washable paint, so I made a decision not to mind.

That night I knew it was time for Dan to be introduced to his new bed and to the idea that he was to sleep in it. Everything was ready. We had played there all afternoon and evening, getting him familiar with the room. We took him to the bath and then went straight to his room. But Dan ran downstairs to the living room.

I sat there on his bed with his wet towel on my lap. Why didn't it work? I did everything right.

But then I reminded myself that Dan sometimes has his own way of doing things. I decided to not give up on my plan.

That night Dan fell asleep in the living room. After he was sleeping deeply, I carried him upstairs to his bed. We didn't know what was going to happen when he woke up in a different place from where he had fallen asleep. But I just had to try. I placed Dan on the bed gently and covered him.

"Please have a good night," I whispered.

As I was about to turn off the light, Tomer appeared carrying his covers. He laid down on the blue rug next to the bed and put his head on the new red beanbag. "I'll stay here all night to make sure he's fine," he said.

I jumped out of my bed at 5 a.m. the next morning. The house was quiet. What had happened? I thought, something must have happened! This couldn't be!

I ran to Dan's room and found him asleep in his bed. Tomer was still asleep as well, on the floor next to him.

You see? Miracles *do* happen. One happened at our house in the fall of 2009.

TEN HOURS A WEEK

September 2009

Even with the sleeping success, times at the new house were stressful. Dan was still uncomfortable and had been crying a lot, and just like after any crisis with Dan, Gali followed with her own disruptions to her otherwise perfect routine. She started waking up at night. Every night at 2 a.m. And she would not go back to sleep till the morning.

After we worked so hard to get Dan comfortable at night in his own bed, I could not let her wake him up. Even with the big house we had now and even with the two of them sleeping in the rooms that were the farthest from each other, there was still the risk of her loud voice waking him. So I would take her downstairs. And from there it was a short way to Cinderella and all the other princess movies. We started watching them in the middle of the night.

I was trying to fall asleep while she was watching the movies but then she would say "Mommy, open your eyes!" and there I was, up and cheering for Cinderella and her prince.

When morning came Gali would fall asleep on the sofa and I would close my eyes, usually for just a few minutes, because then it was time for Dan to wake up. I would leave Gali to sleep on the sofa for an hour and sometimes two and go get Dan ready for school and drive him. Alex would drop Gali off on his way to the train. After a few nights it became my routine. I would fall asleep with the kids at 8 and be woken up at 2 with Gali.

Gali had strange sleep cycles before, when she was younger, so I thought this would not be that bad. After all, she was at daycare and there was a time to nap there. But now Gali was not in the "baby room", and in the "mid-kid room" she had to follow the schedule. She could not just sleep whenever she wanted. So she started having trouble at school too. They would call me to come pick her up because she had been lying on the floor screaming.

Needless to say that between the sleep deprivation, the need to continue to unpack boxes and organize the house, and the daily stress of trying to help Dan, I put my book aside. I hadn't even touched my laptop for weeks.

On one of those crazy days, my uncle called me. He wanted to know how we were getting organized in the new house and to also tell me about his new job. He started working as a sales person at a communication company. He called to see whether I was interested in joining the company as well, as they had chapters everywhere in the U.S.

"No way. You have no idea what my life looks like these days."

"You can make you own hours and the pay could be great, especially once you recruit more people to work under you."

"My own hours these days are packed with Gali waking in the middle of the night and Dan crying during almost every minute from the time he comes home from school."

"What are you doing right now?" It was 11:15 a.m.

"Driving back from the store with groceries. I have to bake Dan's almond bread and make coconut popsicles when I get home."

"And after that?"

"It's going to be time to drive to Dan's school to pick him up."

"And then?"

"Then he'll eat and hopefully play outside on the climber for a while, and then when Gali and Alex get home we'll have dinner. Later I'll give the kids their baths. I'm going to crash into bed at 8 p.m. and at 2 a.m. Gali would wake me up to play."

"And it's like this every day? You're telling me that between all the weekdays you cannot come up with just ten hours to do something for yourself. Even if you worked just ten hours a week, you could still make good money."

After we hung up – I promised him to think about it – I pondered. There must be a way for me to clear just ten hours a week. I was doing a lot and I was indeed exhausted during the day, after being up during the night. But, I could manage my time a bit differently.

Yet if I did have ten hours a week, those hours needed to be dedicated to the most important thing. The thing that I enjoyed most. The thing that filled me with good energy and gave me strength to continue the tough journey I was on. There was only one thing that did all of that for me. My book. That moment I decided to write just ten hours a week. You could say that it was thanks to my Uncle Benny that this book has indeed been written. Otherwise it would have remained an idea – a good one - in my busy, exhausting reality.

THE HOUSEGUEST

September 2009

That weekend we had a houseguest. It was Alex's friend, Eyal, an Israeli law professor whom we were lucky to see every year, when he visited New York.

He arrived on Friday evening and Alex and I decided to take him out and leave Tomer with the little kids. They both went to bed early so we knew Tomer would be fine. I decided to make an effort to put my fatigue aside. Standing in front of the closet upstairs, I wasn't sure whether I should get dressed or perhaps forget the whole thing and put my pajamas on. I was afraid I would fall asleep in the car on the way to the restaurant. Yet I loved spending time with Eyal and I knew this was important to Alex so I put on the best outfit in the closet and came downstairs.

We went to our favorite restaurant and ordered tapas and wine.

"So how are you?" Eyal smiled at me. All he'd seen of me before we went to the car was me running around getting the kids ready.

"I'm good."

He looked at me in silence.

"I mean I've been better. The move was very hard. Dan and Gali are not happy and I'm exhausted. But I'm OK." I picked up my wine glass and drank the chilled white wine. It rolled on my tongue and made my heart beat just a little faster than usual.

"They're just getting used to it, to the house. I'm sure they'll be fine very soon. That's how little kids are."

I nodded and smiled. Eyal has always been so positive.

"And what do you do when you're not running around trying to make everyone happy?"

"I... I've been writing."

"Writing." Eyal looked at Alex surprised. As if Alex should have told him something that important.

"A Book about Dan and autism and this insane journey we are on. I'm just starting. I have a few chapters. I need to get back to it more seriously when things calm down a bit."

The next day we had a nice breakfast and then it was time for Alex to drive Eyal to the train station. We hugged in the kitchen and then he picked up his bag and followed Alex to the door. Alex left first, and as Eyal was walking out he suddenly stopped and turned back to me.

"Send me those chapters you're working on. I'd love to read what you're writing."

And with that simple request he made my book real.

MEETING THE MOVIE STAR

September 2009

The Open House night at Dan's school was coming and I had decided to talk to the Movie Star. He was really successful and he had a kid on the spectrum, at the same school Dan was going to. Which meant that I knew an autism dad who was famous and successful in the industry I was hoping to become a part of. It had to mean something.

The day of the Open House arrived. I woke up with butterflies in my stomach. I asked Alex to cancel class and I had Dara the babysitter arrive early as well. I had to leave the house at 5 pm and I wanted to make sure everything was under control at home. I picked Gali up early, so I could get some time with her before I left. I needed to be as calm as possible. There was no room for anything to go wrong. Not tonight.

It was time to get dressed. I stood in front of the closet. I wore the one pair of jeans that still looked really good on me. I paired it with a dark blue top, with ruffles on the neckline, and my really cool brown boots. It looked nice. It was not too much. I needed to look like my regular self. It would help if he did not show up. At least I would not feel totally ridiculous dressing up. A little bit of mascara and lip gloss and off I went.

In the car, I went over what I was going to say to him in my head. I wanted his help, but I did not want him to feel that I was using the fact that his child was on the autism spectrum to get to him. I wanted to tell him about my book, so he would understand how important it was for it to be published and get to as many parents as possible. How would I do all that in 30 seconds?

I got to the school to find a full parking lot. The beautiful campus was so peaceful in the evening light. The large beautiful oak trees surrounded the lawn like guards and rays of sun caressed the low stone walls that stretched along both sides of the driveway. I could not help but look around in search of a fancy car, which I assumed a movie star must drive.

I walked into the school and was greeted by some of the teachers in the hallway. Most parents were already seated in the large auditorium. They had a talk and they showed a film of the kids busy with their activities so we could see what they are up to at school. It was nice, especially because our kids could not really tell us what they were doing at school. It was partly dark when I walked in, and then they turned off the lights and the movie started. I sat in the back so I could see everyone who was there. There were many dads and two looked like they could possibly be him, by the shape of their heads and hair in the dark. I noted their location and concentrated on the movie. They showed Dan do a puzzle. He completed it in 2 seconds. All the parents said 'wow' but I knew he could do it. That's all he'd been doing at home lately, 48 piece floor puzzles. They also showed Dan riding a pony at the fall festival. I laughed with joy and my eyes watered for a moment. He looked so happy.

The video was over and the lights were turned on. Nope, none of the guys I saw were the movie star. Well, conflict resolved, I thought. At least I wouldn't have to decide now whether to approach him or not. The decision had been made for me. It was probably for the best. After all, what was I thinking? I have been obsessing over this person in my head. He did not even know me. I assumed that because he was famous he could help me make my book into a movie. And there I was excited like a teenager over someone I did not even know.

'I am glad he is not here,' I thought. 'The whole idea was stupid in the first place. He could have completely rejected me and then that would be the end of it. I would feel like my book was rejected, and why? Because a person I did not even know said so?'

The moment came when they divided us into groups. All I cared about the year before was whether Alex and I would get to the speech classroom in time to hear about the hardcore methods they were going to use with Dan. I was afraid to miss it and our babysitter had to leave early for a class. I also really wanted to be with Rachel, Dan's favorite teacher so I could use the opportunity to talk to her a little about how he was doing. This year Alex was not even with me, and all I thought was maybe Movie Star would appear after all, and we would end up in the same group?

We got our stickers. Yes, I was in Rachel's group. We moved to the classroom area and then I saw him. My heart stopped and for just a moment I felt like the world had frozen. And then my heart was beating so fast and I realized I had to decide: Do I chicken out or do I talk to him? He was wearing a baseball cap. That means he does not want to be recognized, right? But what if he just likes that hat or he's having a bad hair day?

Rachel's group started the tour. I knew I had about 20 minutes in each classroom. Three rooms in total, which meant I had about an hour to think about it. The tour was really great. The whole time I tried to listen to what the teachers were saying, but most of the time all I could hear was my heartbeat. Boo-boom, boo-boom.

It was time for refreshments and for the parents to mingle. I went to the refreshment room and there he was, two people behind me in line for coffee. And he took his hat off! There was a big bowl filled with little toys that we were supposed to take home for the kids. They explained at the math classroom that we were supposed to count with them all the time. See, I paid attention! I bent forward and took one for myself and then decided to pass them on to the people behind me. I gave him one too and smiled. He smiled back the nicest warmest smile you can imagine.

I left the room with coffee, a cookie and the heartwarming smile. I did not say a word to him about anything. Outside in the lobby all the moms gathered in a group, talking. I knew almost all of them, and it was so good to see them. Then I saw Movie Star talking to one of the dads. He looked so much like a normal person that I quickly made a decision.

As soon as I noticed that he ended the conversation with the other dad, I took one step toward him and said, “Hey, can I ask you something?”

I started to regret the whole thing, feeling really stupid all of a sudden. But then I heard him say “Sure.” He was smiling his sunny smile right at me and I got lost in his deep ocean blue eyes for a moment. He offered his hand for a shake, “I’m Damien.”

“Oh, hi, I’m Shirley,” I said, my gaze still glued to his eyes. His hand felt leathery and when I looked down for a second I could not help but notice his muscular arms.

“I am working on this book. I am writing it now, about my experience as an autism mom, and it tells all the little stories, and the lessons I’m learning thanks to my son, and I believe that it is different from any book ever written...”

Gina, who I was talking to just before I approached Damien, joined us. He turned to her and offered his hand for a shake.

“Hi, I’m Damien,” he said in his low warm voice.

Gina, who I knew had a serious crush on him, just stood there and looked at him. Unable to talk she pointed to her nametag. But then all of a sudden she found her voice. She nodded at me and said: “I really believe in her book.”

And there he was again, turning the spotlight back on me.

“... and one of my plans is for it to become a film at some point, and I thought that since you’re familiar with the industry.... you might know who I can talk to about this...?”

I finally took a breath. And then I held it in.

He grabbed a pen from the table and a piece of paper and wrote something. “I don’t have a clue what to do at this stage, but email this person. She has experience with the publishing world. Tell her you spoke to me about it, OK?”

He handed me the piece of paper and the name on the email was the same last name as his.

"And hey," he said. I looked back up at him and his piercing eyes were smiling at me. "Good luck!"

***

At the time I didn't realize the real help the Movie Star gave me. For that brief moment, he was a mirror. He was inspiration. He showed me that it was possible to be an autism parents and be successful doing something you love and enjoy.

MEDIATION

October 2009

A few weeks after that, Alex and I met with Laura, the special education director for our town, and her boss. It was time to see if my positive thinking and amicable conversations had translated into a good result. The result we wanted was having Dan placed at Good School.

Before we went to the meeting, I did everything I could to make myself calm and focused. I knew I did not want a fight. I also knew that each side had a chance at winning a case like this in court and we would never know the end result of such a case unless we actually went ahead with it. The only thing both sides knew for sure was how much litigation costs. A lot.

At the meeting we met Laura's boss, 'Ms. Confidence.' She was a very tough lady. As soon as we sat down she said to me, "I understand you came here to try and get your son outplaced to

Good School. I don't think the program there is so good. In fact, I believe our program is better."

She said all that in one long sentence while looking me straight in the eye without blinking.

"Also," she continued, "they always promise the parents that their kids will make such progress in their program, and that soon they will be mainstreamed. Guess what?" She paused. "They stay there for all of their school years."

That statement pierced my confidence. This woman really seemed to know what she was talking about.

I did not get discouraged and I offered mediation as an option. This is a legal proceeding that enables both parties to discuss their goals with a mediator and usually is much cheaper and much faster than litigation in court. They agreed and we scheduled a date. We did this without lawyers present.

The result of the mediation is confidential, just as any such meeting with a district is, so I cannot tell you exactly what was agreed upon. I will just tell you this: our attorney is still working on eating her shirt.

BIRTHDAY PARTY

December 2009

It was time to celebrate Dan's 6th birthday. I felt like we had a lot to celebrate this year. The year before we had a small birthday party, with just my family. My uncle and his family came from Massachusetts and my aunt and her husband came from New York. It was Dan's first year at Good School and we did not know anyone yet. It was before I met the other moms.

Now that we knew everyone and Dan was able to have a good time with his friends at other kids' birthday parties, I decided to go back to my old party planning self and do something fun.

I called Sydney, Dan's OT, and asked to borrow equipment for the kids to play with. I was going to set all the toys in the dining room. Having a huge house to host everyone was great. I invited all the kids from Good School I knew Dan was friends with. It was a large group but I knew they were all going to have fun and that I would have fun with the moms.

I arrived at Sydney's studio early evening that Saturday. All the kids she saw that day had already left. Dan and Gali stayed home with Alex. There was supposed to be a snowstorm so I had to hurry. Yet when Sydney and I found ourselves together in the quiet studio we sat and talked for a while. It was nice. Sydney was the only one who stayed with us all along our journey. We switched speech therapists, we switched programs, but she was still with us. I always valued her work with Dan and her opinion on the other things we were doing for him.

She helped me carry the toys and we filled the back of my car with the trampoline, basketball hoop, large balls and all the other fun bouncy toys. By the last round, snow flakes started falling on our heads. We hurried to hug goodbye and I left.

The storm started to build up on my way home. Before I left, Alex texted me that both kids were already asleep. Perfect, I thought as I was driving slowly, the snowflakes piling on my windshield. I turned on the radio to find that all the stations were playing holiday songs. It was just the beginning of December so I was not tired of these songs yet. I kind of liked it.

I got home to find the house quiet. It was still early so I was not even too tired. We brought the toys in from the car and set them in the dining room. Then went to the kitchen. I warmed us some soup and Alex poured glasses of wine. We watched the white snow covering our majestic street and felt like life could actually be wonderful sometimes.

When Dan and Gali came downstairs the next morning they could not believe their good fortune. The most fun toys ever were in their dining room. We moved the dining table out of the way and they had the whole room to themselves.

Dan's birthday party was a big success. People talked about it for months. The kids had the best time playing with the toys. Some of them got to the other toys and to the DVDs, the house became a complete mess, but it was so much fun I did not care. Dan had the time of his life. He bounced and he played ball. He was happy to see all his friends at his house.

When the party was over and everyone left, Alex said, "Do you realize that we just had a huge party for 15 kids on the spectrum and everyone had fun? There was not even one tantrum, the whole time. How did you do that?"

I stopped cleaning up and looked at him. This party *was* so successful. All the kids and all the parents had fun. I figured that it must have been because the kids felt accepted. Everything was tailored to their preferences. There was no unnecessary noise from music like they have in birthday party places. It was all planned around Dan's needs and they were all like him, so they enjoyed it too.

Tomer said that all the kids were doing so well it was hard to distinguish between the kids on the spectrum and the typical siblings. Until the cake was brought out. And then that picture flashed in my mind. It was true, when I announced the cake all the typical siblings ran to the table. No, wait. All the typical siblings and Dan. He did not mind the many kids around him. He did not mind the noise. He heard cake and he ran to get it. That was something that really warmed my heart. This time Dan could do it. He understood, he wanted to come and he could stand all the other noisy kids around him pushing to get closer to the table.

When Tomer said that, Alex and I smiled at each other, and I knew we were both thinking about that miserable birthday party in New York, back when things were much different. You see nothing is taken for granted in this fragile world of ours.

MEETING TEMPLE GRANDIN

April 2010

The spring after Dan turned six, I reached a very important milestone in my journey to understand the autistic mind. I participated in a conference and heard a talk by Temple Grandin.

Temple Grandin is probably the most celebrated woman with autism in the world. This courageous and hard-working woman overcame autism with the help of her mother and her teachers. She is a doctor of animal science and professor at Colorado State University. She wrote many books and is a livestock industry consultant on animal behavior. She is also known for her books about autism with her ability to provide an inside look at it, and for her work in autism advocacy.

I attended the conference just after I saw a movie about her life. I was fascinated with the way the film showed how Temple Grandin experienced the world in a different way. One scene was especially enlightening for me. They showed her as a little girl sitting with her mother in a doctor's office. She seemed like she was aloof and completely detached from the situation, her gaze fixed on the wall across the room. In the film they could visually show what was the reason she was focusing on the wallpaper. It was because the pattern on that spot did not match the way it did in the rest of the room. That scene reminded me of Dan, and the way he had been staring at wallpapers since he was a tiny baby. There was a restaurant in New York City, where, every time we went, he would sit there fixated on the patterned wallpaper the whole time.

Temple Grandin had the gift of explaining the autistic mind in a way that was very easy for the audience to understand.

"I think in pictures," she said at the beginning of her talk. "When I hear a word my brain pulls out all of the images in my memory that apply to it. It is kind of like a Google image search." Everyone laughed.

This tall, gray-haired woman was very charismatic. She was even wearing the same kind of shirt the film showed her in: a plaid long sleeve buttoned shirt with patches sewn onto it. I sat in the large auditorium with hundreds of parents and professionals and inhaled each and every word she said. She explained what she still experienced sensory overload, and she spoke about her challenges with recognizing people's facial expressions. It was inspiring to hear a detailed explanation of what our kids are going through from someone who was still experiencing it, especially someone who had made a good life for herself.

She also emphasized how important it was that the kids learn how to behave. She indicated that being brought up in the 1950s actually helped her because back then kids had to behave no matter what diagnosis they had. Her mother would make her sit at the table and do all the things she needed to do. The exact opposite of how we are with Dan, I thought.

When we were allowed to ask questions, I was the first to raise my hand. "Do you have any memories from your childhood, Ms. Grandin?"

"Good question." She started marching back and forth on the stage. I was sitting at the edge of my chair, waiting to hear what she was thinking about.

"I remember that one day I threw a tantrum at school and my mother would not let me watch my favorite show on TV that night. My mother and the teacher were communicating all the time, so I could not trick either of them. My teacher knew what was going on at home and my mother knew exactly what was going on at school. After that day, when I could not watch my show, I never misbehaved at school again."

Everybody laughed.

"I also remember being frustrated because people could not understand me sometimes and I could not convey my thoughts to them. Like this one time at school they showed me a card with a picture of suitcases and tried to teach me the word. Now in our house we used to call them bags, and I insisted on saying that to the teacher but she wanted me to say 'suitcases' and that really threw me off. I did not have the words to explain the thoughts that were in my head."

That was helpful. I realized how much Dan must be understanding. I could see that he had a smart brain trapped in a situation where it could not express itself. I also realized how important it was to teach him to behave and show him what's expected of him as a member of society.

THE MOST IMPORTANT WOMAN

June 2010

One of my lessons with Joseph was about my self-confidence. I mentioned a conversation I had at Dan's school and he indicated that I let other people's opinions and beliefs affect me too much.

"Stop letting yourself get carried away."

"What do you mean?" I was truly puzzled.

"You are listening to everyone else too much, and too little to yourself. This is bothering Dan. He needs his mother to be strong and *be there for him.* When you listen to all of those other people, you are giving them too much power over you. It is OK to listen and learn, but you need to take all that in and eventually decide for yourself what's best. When you get carried away, it is as if you are not there energetically, and Dan desperately needs you to be there.

You are his channel to this world. You are what he is leaning on. You need to be strong."

It took me some time to understand what Joseph meant by that. I thought back and realized I always had this dissonance within me. On the one hand I appeared to be the most self-confident person you had ever met, yet on the other hand I always sought everyone's opinions about everything, especially about Dan. Whenever someone mentioned something about him, whether it was a friend, neighbor, someone I met at the grocery store for less than ten seconds, I doubted myself. But he was my son! Now that I saw this problem clearly, I was determined to stop it. I had to go back to trusting my intuition.

***

I had an opportunity to do that when Dan's time at Good School was coming to an end. I was very nervous. Alex and I agreed with our district that after that year, Dan would go to the public school, but I was not entirely comfortable with that plan. When we came to the agreement, it was way back in the winter. I never imagined those months would go by so fast. I thought I'd figure something out when the time came.

And then one day a mom approached me in the parking lot. "Rumor has it Myra the director is leaving to open her own school."

With my back against the wall, I was delighted. I figured that Myra would not be charging the same tuition as Good School, at least not in the beginning. Sending Dan to her school would mean having him taught by the best professional, and it would probably be affordable!

I knew that the news would create madness. Myra was a goddess to all the parents.

We were attracted to her like bears to honey.

Like bees to nectar.

Like autism moms to hope.

If they knew she was leaving, they would follow her anywhere she went.

When the news got out, a few weeks later, my friends were all terrified. They were scared that she would take the teachers with her. The moms were hysterical. Michelle and some other friends were mad that I had not told them as soon as I knew. They were also mad because they knew I was not with them on this, because if Myra left, we would follow her. We were not officially placed by our town like they were.

All of the moms were talking about how when a director leaves the whole school changes. One mom said that her daughter was doing great at a certain school until the director left "and then it all went downhill." Another said Myra had the gift of understanding her child "that nobody else could ever have."

"Why are you so upset with *me*?" I asked Michelle on the phone after she blamed me for not understanding the Myra situation.

"Because you are not getting it. She is really important in the school. I do not know how things will be after she leaves."

"But the school has been there forever, even before she was there, and was still the best in Connecticut."

"You just want her to leave so you will have a solution for Dan next year!"

"Yes, because unlike you, I didn't get my town to pay his full tuition!"

It was bad. As much as I wanted a solution for Dan for next year and really wanted Myra to be teaching him, I did not want to lose my best friend.

A few moms called the owner of Good School and she called Myra. After that talk, I did not know what Myra's plans were anymore.

Michelle called me and reported happily that Myra told her she was not leaving Good School at this point. She sounded so happy and relieved. "People like Myra do not grow on trees, you know."

After I hung up with Michelle I called Myra myself. "The moms told me you are staying."

"Shirley, I didn't say that. You would not believe what happened here today. When the teachers took the kids to the cars they came back shocked. Apparently all the moms were gathered in the parking lot talking about my leaving and crying. One of the teachers came in and told me that. I did not tell Michelle I was staying for sure. I am not staying. I still want to stick to my plan."

Now I was happy and relieved. It was my turn to be on the high end of the roller coaster.

When it was time for Alex and I to go to our PPT, I needed a definite answer from Myra.

"I am going to have an official talk with the management in the morning," Myra promised the day before the meeting.

I was still up in the air.

I called Teresa and told her about everything that was going on.

"You are doing it all wrong again, Shirley," she attacked immediately after I was done. "Why are you fighting so hard?"

"Because we spent all our money and took a loan already. We cannot spend anymore on this."

"That is exactly right. And what do people who cannot afford private schools do? The *regular* people?"

"They go to the public schools. But the public schools are awful."

"Is that so?"

I was afraid to tell her the stories I had heard about public schools. I was scared that if I talked about it, they might come true. Especially the story of the boy who was abused. But then I realized that someone who does not experience autism on a day-to-day basis could never understand the fear involved. However merely being on the phone with Teresa helped me focus. First off, I had to admit I was acting out of fear. I also had to admit I was doing what I was doing because I thought I was protecting Dan.

"If what you were doing was the right thing, you would have found money for it. It was obviously wrong. And the same goes for now. If this new school was supposed to happen, you wouldn't have to fight so hard."

Suddenly the picture of the moms crying in the parking lot came to my mind. Here was a group of women who believed that there was only one person without whom their kids would go downhill. What a ridiculous idea. A child's whole future in one woman's hands.

But then I realized: I was doing the same thing! I believed that Dan would only get better if Myra started a new school and worked closely with him. I was just like those moms. What was I telling Dan with that mentality? And myself?

The most important woman in Dan's life is me. Because I'm his mother and I believe in *him*. And no matter where he is and who is teaching him, he will do well. I believe in his success even if he does not go to the best private school.

I suddenly remembered how Joseph kept on saying that to me when we talked. How I was Dan's channel to the world. How I needed to be strong and stable for him and not be affected by anyone who comes along. "Stop those big movements," he used to say. He meant I should control my thoughts and feelings, but also that I shouldn't be affected by other people so much. I finally realized now how important it was for Dan that I stay strong. At that moment I became empowered.

THE GIRL AT THE BEACH

July 2010

One Sunday morning Alex and I took the kids to the beach. Gali and Alex went into the water together, while Dan and I stayed at our spot. I was sitting on a blanket and Dan was playing in the sand next to me.

Suddenly, Dan got up and walked over to a group of three women who had settled nearby, and stepped on their blanket. I jumped to my feet to apologize but one of them turned her head to me and waved her hand gently as if to say, "Don't worry about it."

I smiled and sat back down, relieved. After a while they went to sit by the water, and to my surprise, Dan followed them there, and started to play in the shallow water very close to them. What could he be thinking? At first I stayed back and watched. But then Dan moved even closer to them, I went down there and tried to tell Dan to stay further away. He wouldn't listen to me, so I decided to sit between him and the group to make sure that he wasn't bothering them. Because he was already so close, I found myself sitting right by their side. As I sat down they all looked at me so I felt like I had to say something.

"I am so sorry he is playing so close," I said quietly, so Dan couldn't hear me. "He is on the spectrum and does not understand the appropriate distance from other people."

One of them removed her sunglasses and smiled. I could tell she was older than the other two. Maybe even their mother.

"He is not bothering us at all. He is welcome here. I have one just like him," she said pointing at one of the girls.

The girl she was pointing at turned her head to me, looked straight into my eyes and smiled. She looked like she was fifteen years old. She had brown hair, dark brown eyes and a beautiful smile.

"No, he is on the *autism* spectrum."

"Yes," the woman, who I now understood to be the mother nodded. And then the other girl, who I soon found out to be the girl's older sister, intervened.

"She was on the spectrum until four years ago. She is fine now."

The mother examined Dan. "He has eye contact. He seems like he is doing well. This one was not at all like that. She was terrible. She would not look at us and she would not talk. She had terrible behaviors. She would bite me and hit me and scream all day long."

I looked at the mother and then at the girl, who was still smiling at me. "So what happened?"

"We did every therapy we could, from the time she was three years old, and at age ten it finally happened. She started talking. We were very lucky. It was God's will."

The girl herself was looking deep into my eyes in silence, still smiling. She looked like a completely typical girl. I did not notice anything. No traces of autism at all. She was sitting there calmly, dipping her feet in the clear water. The ocean was blue behind her and the sky was clear. A few feathery white clouds were resting above us. Light breeze was playing with her hair. I stared at her for a while, unable to speak.

And then I suddenly came back to my senses and realized: I am sitting in front of a person who recovered from autism! This girl sitting in front of me is an immediate channel of information to the subject I was most interested in. My mind started to storm with questions.

"Can I ask you something?"

She smiled and nodded.

"What was it like, the autism? What do you remember?"

"I don't remember much. I only remember that there were things I was doing and I did not know why. I just had to do them. I would line things up. I needed things to be a certain way. I myself don't understand why. And I also remember that I sometimes just wanted to be alone. I don't know why that was happening either. I just felt the need to be by myself."

"She would also do weird things. Remember that thing you did where you were counting with your fingers on your chin. You did that until two years ago or something."

"Yes, I don't know why I was doing that either. It was like I had to. It calmed me down."

"I have a group of parents who have children with autism. I think they would love to hear your story. Would you be willing to come and talk to my group someday?"

"I wish I could, but we live in New Jersey."

"Yes, we are on our way back from visiting family. We were trying to find a beach to stop for a quick dip before we continue our long way home, and we came upon this beach."

I could not believe it. Here was this family that by chance had landed straight on this piece of heaven, on this beautiful Sunday morning, and delivered hope right into my lap. And Dan was the one who found them. How did he know? He wouldn't leave those girls alone from the moment he saw them. He made every effort he could to make me come and talk to them. There was no way to explain this but intuition. He was getting information from his surroundings in a way we simply could not explain. I realized that Dan was also telling me something: Don't lose faith, mommy. I am in here and I will come to you. Just keep believing.

***

The more I thought about that day at the beach, I realized that Joseph's stories about the fairies and rainbows were not common to all autistic people. Joseph saw rainbows. Raun Kauffman saw people's faces floating inside bubbles. Temple Grandin loved to flip things and watch them spin but also understood a lot of what was going on around her. Could it be that every autistic person had their own experience? Maybe the number of possibilities is equal to the number of autistic people? Just like each and every 'typical' person in this world is different.

I realized then that I could stop searching for the magic explanation of how Dan sees the world. He must have his very own special understanding. I know he is smart. I know he understands. I need to start treating him like someone who *can* learn and achieve great things.

***

In the winter of 2013 I was working on finalizing my book. My stepson Tomer, who was visiting from college, offered to listen to me read the whole manuscript. It was a stressful time for our family. After yet another move to a new town, Dan was having a hard time adjusting. We were not sure how to help him. The few hours that Dan was at school, Tomer and I spent reading. Tomer had many good suggestions as we were going over the material. We were having lunch when I got to the part of the story with the girl from the beach. Tomer dropped his fork and looked up at me suddenly. His eyes were glued to mine yet he was partly gazing through me.

"You know, Shirley, when I came for this visit I didn't want to tell you and dad, but I almost lost hope. But now I know that Dan will be OK. This made me remember how he used to be and what potential he has. Our little boy will be fine."

NEW SCHOOL

July 2010

When Alex and I had to go to the PPT, we still had no definite answer from Myra about the new school. After the talk I had with Teresa, and my realization, I arrived at the meeting feeling completely different. There was no fighting planned this time, only planning Dan's program. The meeting went smoothly. Alex and I got to meet Rena, the Board Certified Behavior Analyst (BCBA) who was in charge of the program. She went to observe Dan at Good School and it seemed she had really figured our boy out. The district came up with a good plan tailored to Dan's needs. We felt confident that he would do OK there. We also had no choice but to give it a try.

I asked Rena if she could connect me with other moms who had kids in the program. I knew that connecting with another mom was what I needed. I also wanted Dan to meet at least one of his classmates before the summer program started, so he would have a familiar face.

The next day, Dan, Alex and I went to see the new school. We met Rena again and she explained the method they were using, applied behavior analysis, or ABA. This method is designed to deal with behaviors.

"We reward good behavior and reinforce it, while ignoring negative behaviors to stop them from occurring. When we want a student to stop a behavior, we simply ignore him or make a serious face. When we want to reinforce a behavior, we give a student a desired toy or a treat. They learn that if they do what they are supposed to, they'll get rewarded. You can teach a student many skills that way, including academic subjects."

Rena introduced us to the ABA therapists. We observed them working with the kids and they all seemed wonderful. All in all, the program looked so much better than we expected. Dan stayed with us in the classroom the whole time. When he saw the kids doing a project with paint and glue, he went to join them. This gave Alex and me an opportunity to watch the kids and the therapists for a little longer.

"This boy doesn't even have autism," Alex said to me quietly, nodding towards a sweet blond boy who was at the coloring table with Dan at that moment. "Why is he in this class?"

Rena gave me the phone number of a mom and I called her as soon as we left the school. Elisa, the mom, said she was very pleased with the program. When she told me her son's name I could understand why. She was the mother of the blond boy wc had seen doing so well. Elisa told me that when he started this program he was completely different. The school had helped him a lot.

Dan's behaviors and tantrums did not go away overnight. In fact, in the beginning they escalated. Apparently this is typical when you begin an ABA program. The school sent a team to come to our house and observe Dan. After watching for a few minutes, Rena told us that we must ignore Dan when he was throwing a tantrum. This was new to us. Usually when he was upset, we would try to hug him or offer him something he liked so he would calm down.

"No, don't do that. You would only make it worse. Never reward him with attention when he behaves badly."

I thought about what she had said and it reminded me of what Joseph had been telling me.

"Do not entertain the spirits," he would say. "Remember, sometimes what you see Dan doing is actually the spirits, not him. Learn to ignore them. Do not give them your attention."

Rena and Joseph were explaining a similar tactic. These were two different ways, two different "languages," to explain the same thing.

While ABA helped Dan learn new skills, the public school itself had a big advantage and it had a great effect on Dan. There were typical kids around him. A few months after the year started we got an invitation to participate in the school's community meeting. This was a gathering of all the kids at school. Apparently, Dan was going to receive an excellence award for problem solving in the classroom.

When I arrived for the meeting, I saw a few rows of chairs for the parents of the kids who were getting an award. They picked one student from each class. I sat there in the still empty gymnasium. At exactly 2 pm they started playing music and all the school kids started marching into the room in groups. Even before Dan entered, my eyes watered with joy. The energy in the room felt so good. Like they all belonged to a special community. After all the kids were seated, the principal announced, "And now welcome our V.I.P. students!"

They played the song "Celebrate, good times, come on," and all the kids started to clap to the rhythm of the song. And then the V.I.P students started marching in, Dan among them. The room was crowded and loud, yet Dan walked in with a big proud smile on his face. He got up to receive his award with the help of his one-on-one aide, unlike the typical kids who managed by themselves, but he was completely present and a part of this fun and typical event.

When I left the school that day my heart was bursting with pride. I looked at the trees and the bright blue sky and was thankful for all the goodness that was coming my – and Dan's - way.

GETTING ORGANIZED

January 2011

Dan did very well in the program for a few months. But then in the winter something changed. We were not sure if the problem was something physical, like teeth coming in, or hormonal changes, or whether it was something else.

We reached out to Dr. L., a psychiatrist my friend Gina recommended. As part of his evaluation, he went to observe Dan at school and he also came to our house. On the evening that he came see us, Alex was not there. He was teaching until late that night.

When Dr. L. arrived, he saw the four of us sitting around the dining room table. Tomer was working on his computer, I was sitting at the table with a cup of coffee, and Dan and Gali were coloring with dot-markers. If you've never seen them, dot-markers are little bottles of paint that have a small sponge top. Dan and

Gali loved them and could entertain themselves coloring for hours. While Gali would switch colors and make nice pictures, Dan would stick to one bottle and color a whole page completely on both sides of the paper. Then he would put that away and take another page and do the same. He enjoyed the pounding movement of the dot-marker on the table. Our dining room was quiet besides the toot-toot-toot pounding of the dot-markers and that was interrupted only when Dan didn't find a new page to color on fast enough, and then he would whine.

Dr. L. came inside to this picture.

I introduced the doctor, and Gali immediately left the table to greet him. Dan did not even lift his eyes from the paper to notice something had changed in the room.

"Will you show me your room?" Dr. L. asked Gali. She nodded enthusiastically and went towards the stairs.

"Will Dan come with us?" he asked me quietly.

I went to the table to try and talk to Dan and as soon as he saw my hand reaching towards his paper to move it away, he started to whine loudly.

“I don’t think so,” I looked at Dr. L. with disappointment.

“It’s OK,” he said, and followed Gali upstairs.

Gali showed him her room and then he asked her if she would show him Dan’s room as well. She took him there and he looked quietly at the room. I could see him thinking. It was like he had a computer inside his head that was assessing information from the environment. He nodded while he walked around. Dan’s room was huge. It had two walls with white and blue wallpaper and two walls colored dark blue. Dan’s bed was there and a closet and books, but not many toys. The play area was downstairs in the living room. We did not spend much time upstairs, only when we went to sleep. When I looked at Dan’s room through a stranger’s eyes, it looked so serious.

Dr. L. asked me to give him a tour of the rest of the house. When we were done, he went to the table to say goodbye to Dan. Dan said goodbye without lifting his eyes from the paper. All that time he was still at the table doing the same thing. Toot-toot-toot.

When Alex and I went to see Dr. L. to receive the results of his evaluation, he looked at us and said, "If you ever want Dan to be independent you must stop pacifying him."

At first it felt like an arrow aimed straight at my heart. But then I grasped what he said. Independent. He said that Dan could potentially be independent.

All of a sudden, I did not care about the possibly negative ways we'd handled Dan in the past, according to him. All I wanted to do was change my ways in order to create the future. This was the first time anyone from the medical world had told me there was a possibility Dan would be independent.

Dr. L.'s "prescription" for changing Dan's life was simple. We needed to organize.

"Your whole life is taking place in one room. You are there all the time. You probably eat and play and work all on that table in the dining room, right?"

I nodded. Alex was not sure where this was going, but my mind was already tuned to the same wavelength as Dr. L. and I wanted to hear more. I wanted to know exactly what he saw and how he needed me to change.

"You need to organize Dan's life for him. For your nature it may work to be in the same place at different times a day for different activities, but Dan needs to learn that there is a place to eat, a place to play, a place to learn. This cannot all happen around that same table."

"It's one big mush," I said quietly, partly to myself.

"Yes."

The next day I started. The first thing I did was change the office into a work room for Dan. We were not using the office at all. The room was not even heated, because we were never there. I took all the books and boxes of paper out. I got two small desks with chairs for Dan and Gali. I brought in all the puzzles and toys. I went to a school supply store and got a dry erase board, markers, coloring books with letters and numbers, scented playdough with stamps of letters and numbers. Any and every activity that I thought Dan would enjoy was in that room.

I took the old dining room table and made it into a coloring table. I got a new table that would be used solely for eating.

I cleared all the toys from the living room and bought a big trampoline. I put big balls to bounce on and some hoops too. That spot became the "gross motor area."

Later on, I kept adding techniques to organize Dan and our lives. I used visuals to show him what day of the week it was and what the plan was for that day. My dad got Dan an iPad and I took pictures all the time of what we were doing, so that when we were revisiting a place, I could show Dan a picture to help him remember and understand where we were going.

One day Dan had a tough morning and instead of going to the car with me to go to school, he wanted to play on the slide in the backyard. I showed him a picture of his school on the iPad and said, "First slide, then school." I pointed to the slide first and then to the picture of the school on the iPad. He ran to the slide, went down one time, and then came with me to the car. The system worked like magic. I knew that from then on, I could introduce anything I wanted to teach him, using organizational and visual tools. The world felt much safer to him that way.

The more focused I was on connecting with Dan through visuals, the more creative he became as well. He learned that I could understand him, and he found ways to communicate with me. One Saturday morning Alex and I had a conversation about how we wished Dan would be more independent. Dan took my hand and led me to his bedroom. He went looking through his books on the bookshelf and handed me a book called "All By Myself," about a boy who learns how to get dressed, brush his hair and put his shoes on by himself.

WRESTLING

February 2011

One day in February I came home with Gali after picking her up from daycare, to find a smelly kitchen.

It was a stressful time for our family. Tomer and Alex were busy working on Tomer's college applications, and the stress level was through the roof.

What is that smell? I thought. And then I looked down and saw Tomer's shoes on the floor next to me. It was wrestling season. Tomer was on the varsity team.

I was going to explode, but just then I realized that he actually had followed my rules, and taken his shoes off as soon as he walked into the house.

I went to put my things away and then I smelled that odor again. I looked down to find *my* bag filled with Tomer's stinky clothes from practice.

What? I thought again, this time really angry. But then I remembered that a few weeks before he asked me if he could use it. I did not know it was going to be this stinky when I said yes. It was a travel bag that I bought in New York back in the days when I was working in the law firm and could afford almost anything I wanted.

Oh well, I thought. I'll have to find a really good way to clean it.

Gali took her coat off and we went into the dining room to find Alex sitting in front of piles of papers. He was so focused on it, that he barely noticed us when we came in.

"Where is Dan?" Alex gave me the look of 'I don't know.'

I was sure Tomer wasn't with him. I thought I'd find him sitting by his computer, busy on Facebook! He probably hadn't even taken a shower yet!

During this stressful time, he'd been doing that a lot: sitting on his computer chatting with friends. Sometimes I felt like we didn't exist to him. He never sat with us for dinner anymore, because he only ate an apple a day, so he could make weight for his wrestling matches. The only time he spoke to me or Alex was when he wanted something.

By the time I got to the living room to find Dan, I was furious. I felt like there were flames coming out of my head.

I was about to explode, when all of a sudden I heard laughter. It was Dan laughing. When I walked in I saw Tomer, his hair still wet from the shower, wrestling with Dan on the carpet. I stayed and watched and saw that he was teaching Dan how to wrestle.

"Say Fireman," Tomer said.

"Fireman," Dan said, and then Tomer did the wrestling position with him.

Dan was delighted.

I took a step back and went into the dining room to see Alex and Gali. What I had just seen was too good to interrupt.

THE YOUNGER SISTER

March 2011

One of the biggest gifts Gali brought into our lives, aside from being the most wonderful, creative and lovely girl, was that she grew up with Dan by her side and did not know that he was different. As a toddler, when we would go somewhere together, she would draw his attention to things. "Dan, look at the water!" she said on one of our trips in the car passing by a lake. Alex and I looked at each other and smiled. Alex and I made sure to facilitate the communication between her and her brother, by answering for him. When Gali was three years old, it was very clear to her that Dan doesn't talk. He was six at the time, and was able to request things, but he could not have a conversation with her, unlike her friends from daycare.

When Gali was four, Dan was going through a period of "behaviors." Dan would go and grab the toy Gali had been was playing with, or worse, her favorite blue blanket, and run off. Gali would then scream and Dan would laugh. Alex and I felt that he wanted to play with Gali, but he did not know how, so that was the method of communication he adopted. Gali, however, was terribly bothered by this behavior. Not only did her brother not talk to her, but he was taking her things as well.

It was years before we started to really explain autism to her. But back then when we did not know exactly how to approach it, I made a creative attempt.

One day when Gali was taking her bath, she asked me to tell her a story. I didn't have any particular idea for a story, so I decided to make one with her.

"Once upon a time there was a giant, named..."

"Soup."

"Yes, Soup. And he lived in the woods."

"And everyone was scared of him!"

"Because he couldn't talk."

"Yes! He couldn't talk at all."

"And one day he took all the stars away from the sky, and everyone was scared in the dark and angry at him."

Gali listened quietly, her wise green eyes looking deeply into mine.

"He took the stars and packed them in his dirty sack. He then carried that heavy sack into the woods, his steps pounding loudly in the dark forest, and for some reason he went to a big oak tree and removed it from the ground! Soup then poured all the stars into the hole that formed under that tree. Suddenly everyone in the woods heard many little voices screaming 'Hurray!'

"Because under that tree there was a cave, and there were lots of little dwarves stuck in there, and they couldn't find their way out because it was too dark. Nobody knew that the dwarves were there because nobody could hear them, but soup's ears were so sensitive that he could hear them. When he poured the stars into the cave, the stars drove the darkness away and the dwarves could see their way out."

"Mommy," Gali looked at me very seriously.

"Yes, Love?"

"Soup was not mean like everyone thought he was."

"That's right, Honey."

"In the beginning they did not understand him, but afterwards everyone knew he was good!"

***

For years we would talk to Gali about Dan and his friends, we used to call it "children who cannot talk." When she was in kindergarten, I bought a few books for her about siblings of children with autism. Some of them were written by siblings. After we read those and the more she met siblings of Dan's friends, she realized that she was not alone in her situation.

Most times she is very brave. She learned that sometimes our whole family needs to leave public places abruptly because Dan cannot take it and we are afraid he will have a tantrum. She learned to live with times that Dan did indeed throw a tantrum, sometimes in the presence of her friends. Alex and I always tried to soften things for her and compensate her afterword by going somewhere else, but it was not easy.

The older Gali gets the closer she is with her brother Tomer. Those two have something very big in common and it is just one more thing that glues them together, besides their love for each other and their shared traits, such as creativity, love of music and being silly sometimes.

One night I was waiting for Gali to wash her hands after going to the bathroom and she asked me whether she could have a little brother. Gali's best friend from kindergarten had one, and she wanted one too.

"I don't know if we should have another brother. We have an older brother, Dan, already. Why don't we wait until you are older and have your own baby?" I made a joke.

Gali stopped and looked at me through the mirror very seriously. And then she started to cry. She was sobbing and shaking. I hurried to hold her tight. "What's wrong?" I asked while hugging her close to me, feeling her little body shake and her breath choking.

"What if my baby doesn't know how to talk?"

I realized that my smart daughter was so aware of what I have been going through. How strong she was for carrying on with her life the best she can despite the abnormalities in our family. How she learned to cope so beautifully. Yet how much this difficulty weighs on her little shoulders.

I picked her up, still in my hug, and carried her to her bedroom. I sat us both gently on her purple quilted cover. I dried her tears and brushed her hair back.

"Gali, this will not happen. It will be a long time before you are a mother. They will find something by then to help all those kids who cannot talk. And your baby will talk. I promise you."

She calmed down slowly in my arms and we read a book together until she fell asleep.

A few weeks after that I attended a parent-teacher conference with Gali's kindergarten teacher and received the surprise of my life.

There were two special needs boys who had been integrated into Gali's class. They were pulled out for their therapy, but they spent a lot of time in class. It turned out that Gali "adopted" them both as her good friends and would organize games at recess with these two boys. She always included her other friends too, and they would all laugh a lot while playing. My sweet little girl was passing it forward.

***

To this day Dan has behaviors that annoy Gali.

"It makes me angry to be with people who can't talk."

Yet sometimes a ray of sunshine comes down to our house and we have a day when she wakes up full of love and compassion. We had a day like that just before I sent this book to print. Gali woke up and hung out with me in the kitchen until it was almost time to go to school. I was making a story on Dan's iPad, so he could tell his teachers at school about his weekend. This time we had gone to a farm. Gali helped me by telling me what I should write under each picture. "We went into the corn pit"; "we climbed the hay stack"; and "Gali fed the goat."

Then she took the iPad to go show Dan the story we made. She climbed onto his bed and removed the blanket from Dan's face. She sat there reading the story to him page by page. He listened to her and smiled. He stayed quiet the whole time. I stood outside the door and prayed that one day every day would be filled with moments like this, peaceful and full of love.

AUTISM PARENTS COMMUNITY

April 2011

Two years after I first met my autism mom friends, I decided to throw a very special party for our group: an autism-zumba-party. I came up with the idea in the middle of a zumba class. The dance studio I was attending was spacious, well lit and was dressed from floor to ceiling with beautiful lively colors. The owner, Mary Rose, was a wonderful zumba instructor and a very charming lady, who hosted fundraisers and supported the community in many ways. I knew they were having kids birthday parties there, but I did not know how she would react to my idea of having an autism-zumba-party. I did not think anyone had done that before. After pondering for a while, I finally approached her and asked.

Mary Rose looked at me with her deep blue eyes and I could barely breathe from the anticipation. My heart was beating fast.

"Sure," she finally said. "What do you need?"

I dried the tears of joy that were running down my cheeks and told her how I thought it should work: the volume of the music had to be lowered because most of our kids were sensitive to sound; the kids would need time to get used to the space before we started any activity; the dances should be as simple to follow as possible; and we should expect that some of them will not be able to join us and that would be fine.

Mary Rose wrote down everything I said and circled the date in her calendar. I emailed my friends and invited them to the party. I also emailed a mom who had a mailing list for autism parents in CT so it would reach the whole community.

On the morning of the party, I woke up with butterflies in my stomach. I was excited yet I was worried: What if people didn't show up? What if the kids didn't participate? What if they ran around screaming and banging their hands on the mirrors? What if someone got hurt? What if Dan could not enter the studio?

When we arrived at the party Dan happily went in. I sighed with relief. The music was playing in the background at a very low volume. Gali and Dan walked around and were checking their reflection in the big mirrors. They both seemed to like the place. I was glad we made it early enough. When the time for the party came I looked at Mary Rose nervously. She smiled at me. My friends began to arrive with their families. Within minutes the studio was filled with kids running happily and parents walking around smiling.

Dan found himself a new friend. He was an older boy who was running around and dancing and Dan simply joined him. Gali's friend from school arrived and Gali joined her and her parents on another side of the room. I saw them spinning like princesses and checking how high their skirts would rise. Everything was so relaxed and under control.

Mary Rose made name-tags for the kids and when it was time to start I panicked for a minute. I looked at my friends and they all smiled at me, reassuringly.

Mary Rose turned the volume up just a little bit to get everyone's attention and told us to stand in a big circle. She started introducing zumba moves to warm up. The moms started to imitate her and to my surprise some of the older kids did too. While some children chose to run around the studio, Dan stayed with me in the circle.

After the warm up they put the 'hokey pokey' on. To my surprise, Dan attempted to follow the moves of the dance. I did not even know he knew that one! That day was just full of surprises. Mary Rose and the other teachers were introducing more dances and Dan let me move his arms and danced with me. At some point I hugged him and held his hand in a tango position and we walked and danced like that around the studio. He enjoyed it so much that he wouldn't let me go. He kept on dancing, with a big smile on his face the whole time. The other kids had a great time as well. Everyone got to participate when they wanted and do their own thing when they needed to. It was the best party ever.

Before they left, my friends came and hugged me. We all felt like we reached a new level of enjoyment with our kids. Parents I did not know before came to me to thank me for the great time. I got emails later telling me how much the kids enjoyed it and how this was a first for them too, dancing with their children.

The success of the party and the reaction I got from parents convinced me that this is something people need and are truly missing: an opportunity to enjoy themselves with their children, doing things that typical kids do, in a safe environment. All we did was lower the music and have loving teachers show them how to dance.

After thinking more about this concept, I formed a new organization in Connecticut: Autism Parents Community. I figured that there were so many parents who were not as lucky as we were, to find each other, come out of the isolation, and enjoy life together. I wanted people to know about us so they could join us if they were around or be inspired to form their own group if they lived far away. I built a website and posted my story, and described how my life changed after I met the other autism moms.

Later on, I created more events like this one, where children and parents could enjoy themselves in a safe, non-judgmental environment. We had so many zumba parties since that first successful one. Now the kids can actually follow the zumba moves! I contacted the local cinema and we are having special sensory screenings, where the volume is lowered and the lights stay slightly on, so the kids will be more comfortable.

We make sure to make plans during school vacations. We are continuing to have fun together as a community. Our focus is always on what our children *can* do.

After I put the videos from our parties on my website I was invited to participate in the morning show on TV. They wanted to create awareness for my organization. They said they had two seats so I could bring someone with me, preferably a child. I decided to bring Dan. It was a morning show on Saturday. We had to be there at 6 a.m. I woke up at 5 a.m. to get ready. At 5:30 I woke everyone up. It was still dark outside yet with my high energy and excitement and with Alex's help, we got the kids ready in twenty minutes and we drove together to the TV station, which was located ten minutes from our house. We entered a room full of screens and I showed Dan the woman who was about to interview us. We then entered the actual studio where more people were waiting their turn to be interviewed. Dan got so excited that he started to run around. I decided to take him out of there, but he must have understood the importance of this and so he refused to come out. He really wanted to be there! By the time it was our turn he was so excited. For a second he sat on the chair next to the anchor but then he started to run around the studio. After a while, when someone tried to stop him, he started to whine.

On live TV. I was sitting there with the anchor trying to concentrate and answer her questions yet what I really wanted was to go to Dan. They must have managed to call Alex and he was trying to get Dan out of the studio to no avail, because Dan did not want to leave the scene. I could see on the anchor's face that she was receiving directions through her headphone to cut our interview short. She asked me two more questions and that was it. My screen time was over. I was completely OK with it. I got to say some of what I intended; they showed a segment of the video from one of our zumba parties; and Dan was happy for a few seconds so people could see how adorable he is. It was Dan who was sad when we had to leave. He didn't realize that the interview was supposed to be short. He thought he did something wrong.

"You did good, Dan," I bent down and sat on my knees next to him. "That's how TV is. You come in for a few minutes and you leave."

He calmed down and we left.

Soon after that appearance, the New Haven Register did an article about my organization. Sandi, the reporter came to my house. I told her about my work with the autism community. I told her about how we support each other and how when I was having trouble with Dan one day, a mom came to me and said, “How can I help you? What do you need? I have two of my own, I get it.” And just telling her about this made me cry again.

“It’s the kindness that kills us, right?” the reporter smiled at me, and I knew we would be friends forever. And it wasn’t just that. Sandi also turned out to be a great teacher and a big support for me and my writing.

After the article came out, I received hundreds of letters from parents from all over Connecticut. People told me they felt so lonely and they were so happy to have an opportunity to belong. People were also so excited and touched by the way my organization saw children with autism, as individuals who *can*.

These letters moved me into organizing workshops I called “get into your child’s head.” I asked Myra to give a workshop about how children with autism perceive speech. I asked Sydney to give a workshop about the sensory system and how to help our children overcome the overload. My friend Sally gave a talk about ear health, something so important for so many of our children who are sensitive to sounds. And my workshop was about managing stress in order to communicate with our children better. I explained the concepts Joseph had been teaching me and conducted a meditation session. It felt wonderful to share Joseph's wisdom with others and to see how happy and relaxed they felt when the evening was over.

FORGIVENESS

May 2011

One day I saw Mrs. Stern, the director of Dan's first preschool in Connecticut, at the Italian Market. I used to go there often to get prepared foods and Italian cookies. This market is a very popular place. It is close to Gali's daycare and I would often run into someone I knew, usually other parents who lived around there. I was usually by myself so I could chat with them while waiting in line in the tiny space between the shelves.

But that day I was not alone. I came with Dan. And that made the experience completely different. Because with Dan in public I had to always expect the unexpected. I never knew which direction he would pull me in. And I usually needed to pray that he would let me get everything I needed before he demanded to leave. This comes with the territory of travelling in the autism lane.

Lucky for me, I managed to get everything I needed and get in line at the register. Dan was checking out the cookie stand, which was not too far from the register. So I could stand in line and he was still pretty close to me. I knew I was going to get whatever he chose for himself. That was a given when you went food shopping with Dan.

And then she came in. Mrs. Stern. She simply pushed the door open and walked into the store. I hadn't seen her in those four long years since we left her school.

For a split second our eyes locked. And then I had to make a choice. Because there were a number of things I could do at that moment.

I could lower my head and pretend I did not see her. For a long time in my life that is what I did: pretended that this woman did not exist and that everything she said to me did not exist either. You could call it denial. I called it hope.

But that day at the Italian market, my life was already different. It was after I'd met my autism mom friends and we created a universe of our own. I no longer felt like I was cast out.

I could also talk to my friends about people like her, who were intimidated by our kids. We would always say that we ought to smile at those people instead of lowering our eyes. You know that those who do not smile are the ones who need a smile the most. We held our heads up and we smiled. We learned to be proud of our children, just the way they were.

We also knew that we had to forgive these people because being angry only hurts us. It is energy blocking our way to happiness. I had been working on it for so long, trying to forgive her. But thinking about her in theory was not at all like seeing her in person, with Dan!

So when Mrs. Stern saw me, I looked strongly into her eyes. "Hello," I said, and smiled.

She looked like a deer caught in the headlights. She looked as if she would like to turn back and run through the door. But I guess she decided to be brave too, because she stayed inside the store.

"Hello," she finally replied. "How are you? How is Dan doing?"

"Oh, he is actually right here." I pointed at Dan who was luckily very calm and looked pretty typical still standing in front of the cookie shelf deciding what he wanted to have.

"He has grown so much," she said.

"Yes, can you believe this is the same little peanut who went to your school?"

Then it was time. I had to decide whether I was ready. If I could take the extra step that would release me from this forever.

"You know," I said quickly before she went further into the store. Before I could change my mind. "I have been thinking about you lately. About how you gave me a kick a few years ago," I stopped for a second, "a kick in the right direction."

She looked at me, surprised. I could tell she had not expected this. That moment I realized that she must have been thinking about that incident too. It must have been so unpleasant for her as well. Especially after she tried to help us, in her way. She talked the professionals into accepting us sooner for an appointment because the sooner you begin treatment the better it is for the child.

In my head I had accused her of doing this so she could get the evaluation reports quickly and have a written backup to get Dan to go to a different school. Looking in her eyes now I realized I must have been at least partially wrong.

“Wow,” she said and shook her head, bringing herself back from my shocking statement. “Well, good luck. It looks like you are doing a good job with him.” She nodded at Dan.

I looked at him and my eyes watered. This time I was unable to look her in the eye. Because even though this comment may sound so technical, coming from this tough lady it meant simply the world.

***

After that meeting I felt a big relief. To use Joseph’s visual, that incident released a big block of energy from my channel.

As years go by I still meet people like Mrs. Stern along my journey. Sometimes they are educators. Sometimes doctors. They focus on how different our children are from the normal and not on the beauty and special gifts our children have. I used to get angry with them, until I learned that this is a matter of perspective.

When such perspective bothers me I know that there's something inside of me that needs forgiving. It is always the hardest to forgive yourself. I sometimes still feel like I should have done things earlier, and that I could be doing more for Dan even now. Many years of spiritual work have made me understand that it was not me who did this, and yet I still need to remind myself that on a daily basis.

THE FAMOUS AUTHOR

April 2012

All that time, in addition to organizing events, writing a blog, and taking care of Dan and the family, I kept working on my book. Every time I talked to someone about my writing, people showed an interest in it.

When I finished the first three chapters, I shared them with three people. Nira, my good friend from law school in Israel, Liat, my good friend from New York, and Eyal, Alex's friend.

When I finished my first draft, I shared it with Marcy, Nina, and Blair, three dear, lovely ladies I met at a conference I attended with Alex. We formed a little group while our husbands were at the conference, and I told them about my writing. On the last day of the conference, they all approached me and asked me to send them a draft. At that time I had 20,000 words of the first draft (I didn't know I would end up having about twenty five drafts by the time this book was ready for print) and their request encouraged me to send them the book so I got very serious about writing it!

The feedback I got from my "readers" was overwhelming to me. They all thought the story was very good. They had comments and suggestions, which I appreciated, because I knew that the more eyes the better my book would become. My friend Liat, who volunteered to edit the manuscript for me would comment on different parts. Almost every page had a "wow!" on it and sometimes she would write, "Now I'm crying..." She also told me that thanks to the book she understood what I was going through as an autism mom so much better. This was in spite of the fact that we were on the phone almost every single day, and I thought I had involved her with everything that was going on. I only became more encouraged to push forward and finish my book, so more people who have an autism mom in their lives would be able to understand her better.

One day Alex had an idea. He told me that he was thinking about approaching a famous author he knew. And when I say famous I mean a very famous and successful author. One of his books was an international best seller. It was adapted into a film that was nominated for six

Academy Awards - including for the screenplay - and got a very famous actress her first Oscar. Alex asked him to read my manuscript and give me comments, and he agreed.

I was so excited that someone like him was willing to read my work. I did not expect him to do it very fast, because I figured he must be a busy man and that he had been flying back and forth to Europe. Yet, after just a few weeks, he emailed me back. He finished reading my manuscript and shared his opinions and comments with me. I could tell that he was sincere when he was writing about the parts he loved. He gave me the most helpful advice about aspects he thought could be improved. I was very excited to get his feedback. The fact that someone like him even read my work was tremendous to me. Who could imagine he would say it was good?

I wrote back to thank him and invited him to come visit us here in CT on one of the weekends. He wrote back immediately that this would probably be hard to arrange because of his tight schedule, flying back and forth to Europe and being tied up with other engagements. My heart sank as I was reading his email, but them he added: if you can, why don't we meet up in the city?

I did go to the city once in a while, but even if I didn't, I would go for this! We made a date to meet and my excitement went through the roof.

I decided to read his book again before we meet. My old copy was in Israel so I ran to the store to get a new one. The guy at the information counter knew immediately which book I was talking about. He quickly took me to the right shelf and handed the book to me. When I saw the cover I got chills. I did not know that it got *so* many excellent reviews. Both the front and back covers listed praise from the New York Times, Los Angeles Times, and more U.S. and European newspapers.

I started reading it immediately and within just the few first lines was consumed again by the story and the characters. I could visualize them and their surroundings so clearly. It felt like I was with them. I was reading so fast not because of the short time I had until the meeting, but because I could not bear the thought that I would have to put it down and engage in my regular life. Each moment I had until the time of the meeting I spent with them, with his characters: their love, happiness, sadness, anger and fears. I was there with him, frustrated, when she disappeared and I was heartbroken when their fate brought them together again under tragic circumstances.

I saw his female character clearly before my eyes and I could fully identify with his male character when he realized that he was the only one who understood her. I knew this frustration very well. It was the same as when I felt like I was the only one who fully understood my Dan. His female character could talk, yet she was illiterate in the intellectually based culture of Europe of the 1950's and 1960's. This was probably like having autism in America of 2012. She could not truly engage in the world around her, just as Dan can't today.

I barely managed to finish the book on the train to New York. Still sobbing from the emotional ending of the story, I ran to catch the subway on my way downtown.

I arrived at the restaurant and waited for him inside. I loved the place he picked for us to meet. It was both elegant and warm. I was not sure how I'd recognize him. All I had was an old picture from the back cover of the book. I finally saw him arriving. He was tall with silver gray hair. He wore a long, black, belted coat.

We sat down and he told me how much he loved my story and the way my characters were developed. He asked me more questions and gave me some suggestions. He was interested in hearing more about my plans to revise my book.

I told him I was working with a writing coach who encouraged me to make my book a how-to book, "how to cope after the diagnosis" kind of book. I told him that although she had some suggestions, I did not feel like I could put myself at a position to give other people advice. "I'm still learning myself," I laughed.

"It's always better to convey your messages through a good story," he agreed.

"The thing is, she is working with an agent, so if I do what she says, I may get a foot in the door with this agent. It is so hard to get a book published here."

"I wouldn't know a thing about this. My book was published in my country in my language years ago. I'm sorry it is so hard these days. But I'm sure you'll find a way. When something is good, it finds its way out."

Then we turned to talk about him. I asked him how it happened that his book was picked up to become a film.

"I'm not sure," he said. "After it was on Oprah's favorites list they simply called me. They looked me up and found me in Europe. We had to choose a studio and a director and I got to participate in all that. It was fun."

How humble was he. He was telling me this the way he might tell me about a walk that he took in the park. Simple. Descriptive.

"What's your next project?" he asked me.

I told him about my idea for the second book and his eyes widened. I told him how it will be a true fiction yet it will include scientific facts and a legal theory that is novel and that Alex and I developed together, thanks to my obsession with autism and frustration at not knowing its cause.

"This book will be brilliant. I can feel it," he said.

We talked about everything after that. About Dan and Gali and his family at home. It felt like I had a new friend, but one I had known forever. He was so warm and I was enjoying the rays of light he was sending in my direction.

"I have a feeling that you will make it big," he said to me when we hugged goodbye, and I could envision him saying "Kid, you got this," just like one of his characters used to say to the other.

DREAM

They take pictures of mountain climbers on top of the mountain. Nobody wants to know what happened before they got there. Same goes for autism stories. Everyone is interested in the ones about "victory." The moms who beat autism get the spotlight. This story is for the moms who are still climbing the mountain. It is steep, it is hard, and many times it is ugly.

One of the comments I received about my book was that I did not expose enough of what we're going through with Dan. It is very hard to explain the challenges. The unpredictability of life, the helplessness of not being able to help your child when he is in pain, your child's frustration when he is not understood. I guess unless someone is at my house during a tantrum they will never fully understand. I hope I was brave enough in sharing aspects of the lives we autism parents lead, in order for the world to know what we're going through.

When the challenges were weighing heavy, I had to remind myself that I am not solely Dan's mother. I am a wife, a daughter, a granddaughter, a sister, an aunt, a stepmom, a friend, and a mom to my Gali.

I also had to remind myself about my own dreams and wishes.

***

The writing of this book has been therapeutic for me. It started as a compilation of experiences that expressed the feelings I had at the time. The book and I grew together. Layers of buried emotions that were inside of me were exposed writing these stories. The more I expressed my fears and doubts the better I could handle them. The more I wrote and rewrote and then added and changed yet again, the deeper I reached inside of me, the more aware I became and the better I eventually felt.

I found what I've learned on this writing journey gave me the tools to perform all the tasks I was facing and – most of the time – maintain peace during what in the past seemed like complete chaos.

I wish I didn't have to work so hard to achieve those understandings. I wish I had this book handed to me after Dan was first diagnosed. Think of it, I need this book even now during hard times! This is what I need in order to remind myself of the gift I've been given in the form of this beautiful boy. Without him – and his challenges – I wouldn't know what I know today and I wouldn't be able to write about it. He was the reason I started writing in the first place.

If you are reading these lines you know that I made my dream of publishing a book come true. What is your dream?

Blog Post from my website May 11, 2012:

CONVERSATION WITH GOD ON A RAINY DAY

"God," I said one morning last week, when nothing seemed to be going the way I wanted, "I usually spend my mornings thanking you for all the wonderful things you have given me, but today I can't help but ask you: Why? Why me? Why do I have to face all this difficulty? Why can't I get anything I want? Why is my life so hard?"

"Hard?" said God, "why what do you mean?"

"I mean why is it taking me so long to get my book published? It's such a good book and you know it. It should have been out there by now, hopefully a best-seller."

"Oh did you finally send it out to publishers?"

"Well, I'm talking to this agent and she mentioned it to some people..."

"You remind me of this guy," God said, "who keeps praying to me 'I wish to win the lottery please God,' but he never buys a ticket! How can I get your book out if people don't have your manuscript?"

"Once I send it out you'll make it big right?"

"My dear, everyone on your planet wants this: to be big. If I created every creature and plant big, you wouldn't have flowers and grass. You would only have tall trees coming out of the ground. And there would only be elephants walking around. No birds and butterflies."

"But there are some elephants out there. Please make my book an elephant! How soon can that happen?"

"What's the rush?" God said, "You all want everything *now*. You can't wait for anything. I'm very puzzled by this. You all know on a deeper level that time doesn't matter. Before you come onto this planet, I show you that. How everything actually exists at the same time, and "time" as you treat it is only an invention to organize your lives and nothing more. Yet you all forget this the moment you leave me and go there, and you get confused. Remember that everything you want you have already been granted. Just let things come to you in their own time."

"God," I asked after a pause, "why does my boy still have autism? Why doesn't he talk yet? I've done so much. I work so hard on getting him the right program at school. I get him the best therapy. I go through hoops to find the best doctors and the best treatments. I've done it all, yet he still has such a long way to go. Why, God?"

"Did you just hear yourself?" God asked me, "*He* still has a long way to go. I've been watching you do all those things, be sure I have. And I really applaud you. You are pretty amazing. I don't know if I could do such a great job, really. But you are forgetting that this is only partly your journey and mostly his. You can't ask me to do that: get involved with his progress, for *you*. It is a course that he chose before he came here. It's not yours to touch. And you know," God continued, "I'm still cracking up when I hear this word: 'autism.' What do those doctors even mean? They created this name and they treat it as if those beautiful children have an illness when all they really have is the gift of being open to higher levels of understanding. Do you know why there's so many "cases of autism," like you call it? Why the numbers keep growing? It's because the people on your planet are evolving towards a better understanding of the universe. You are starting to be open to the greater wisdom, as opposed to being busy with a need to physically survive and fight over pieces of land. The people are starting to understand that your planet is not the only one and that you are a part of something much greater. The children who take upon themselves the mission of teaching come here with "an illness" and by that they are awakening their environment. You better start seeing your son as a leader, instead of sick. Then you would not ask when his "sickness" will disappear. You will appreciate his knowledge and the task he took upon himself."

"There is a big difference for me between having him labeled as "autistic" which I don't mind that much anymore, and having to watch him suffer. You know how many times he is in pain and I can't help him?

"Why do *I* of all people have to sit there and watch my son suffer? I met my neighbor yesterday and she has five children and they are all healthy and normal. She just travels this earth in peace raising them! When they are at school she goes to community meetings and has coffee with friends. She entertains all the time. Why not me?"

"Now you are bringing back history again. Remember when you were about to come to this planet and we were browsing possible paths for you? I told you that I cannot guarantee exactly what you will get but you can make a few wishes about the life you are about to experience. Remember what you told me? You said: just not boring. Whatever you do, I do not want a boring life. And here you are. Are you honestly telling me you would rather have your neighbor's life instead of yours? Would you be able to raise five children and not have your own career, goals, ... life?"

I thought for a minute and then said quietly: "You know my answer to that. No. I prefer this. But why can't my goals and career happen already? I am working so hard. I spent so much time writing this book and revising it and then revising it again. Why can't my voice be heard? Why can't I get it published? Why can't I go on TV or something to promote it? Why, God?"

"If all of your people were on the stage, who would be there to watch?"

"But it makes me sad to work so hard and wait so long. It's like a rain that never ends and I am forced to sit inside and never come out."

"Rain is not bad," said God, "I created it in order to water the flowers and trees. Have you noticed how bright and lively they look after the rain? It is a good thing to rest and nourish oneself. Afterwards, things actually grow better and higher."

"But why not grow faster?"

"That again?" God laughed, "If I removed the dirt and pulled out seeds that I have just planted to make them grow faster, I would destroy them. I need to water them with rain and wait. So do you.

"How about some perspective?" God added, "You have a roof over your head. You are never hungry, unless you go on one of those stupid diets of yours because you don't trust that I made you beautiful enough. More than half the population on your planet doesn't have a roof and food whenever they want."

"I get it," I said slowly, "I really do. You taught me so much today."

"Look, I got to go," God said, "but I promise: your things are coming."

"Ok," I said, "but please hurry, God!"

EPILOGUE

My son Dan is taking me on an amazing journey. It's hard, it's unpleasant, a lot of time it is cold, lonely and dark. Many times I feel like hopping onto a comfortable tourist bus, instead of trekking with him on the difficult roads he chooses. But then sometimes we reach a high point and we are on top of a mountain and I can see things that I couldn't if it wasn't for him. I challenge myself and it feels good. I challenge myself to find strength that I didn't even know I had. And thanks to him I have to search and reach those deep, deep places that I would not tour otherwise. And when we stand on top of mountains and look around, and everything is clear and everything is bright, and you can see the future, that's when I know how rewarding this is. And I know that the road to the next top has to go through trails and valleys down below, and it's going to be hard. Yet I know he will take me where I need to go and I'll take him where he needs to go, and we will be able to reach that next top together.

***

The biggest lesson Dan taught me was acceptance. Accept him. Accept myself. Accept the world around me, including the spirits I used to be so scared of. Because everything around me is a part of *me*.

I cannot control everything, but I can control myself. My perception is what creates the world around me. By applying the right perspective, I align everything. And once I do that, it ripples to people around me.

I have watched over the years how Dan changed everyone he came in contact with. He changed all of us. Thanks to him I can see the depth of Alex's commitment to fatherhood and his connection to his children. I can see what a responsible and loving young man Tomer had become. How Gali managed to find that delicate balance of having a 'typical' life yet a part of her very special family. My parents, my sisters, and everyone in my extended family are learning new perspectives thanks to Dan.

There are so many children like Dan around the world. So many moms. So many dads. So many families. Each home in each country may speak a different language, yet all of us share one language: autism.

Dear Dan,

I have just finished my book. The book about you, about us. I told our story, the story of our journey.

I told about how we started our journey and how scared we were. I told about how much I learned in the process. What you have taught me. Because Dan, I have had many teachers in my life. But you are by far the most important one. You moved me from my padded comfort zone and showed me what was truly important.

There were things in the book that were easy to tell. Like how successful I felt the closer I got to solving the puzzle. The puzzle of how to help you.

But the hardest part was telling how I learned to appreciate the little things life has to offer. Like when we sit together and you look into my eyes and smile. I appreciate these moments so much because it took me so long to get them.

I will never take for granted that you are calm and happy. Every word you manage to say lights up my world.

In the future, when you get your feelings hurt playing with a friend, while I comfort you like any mom would do, I will also cheer in my heart, because I will know you understand friendship and long for it.

If when you are a teenager you ever say, "I hate you mom!" I will cherish it. Because at some point it was not even clear you would ever make a conversation.

If, when you are in high-school you get mad at me while completing college applications, I will celebrate.

When you graduate from college, I will throw such a big party and invite everyone I know.

But until all of this happens, I will celebrate each and every moment I have with you, my love.

Because regardless of my dreams for you happening one way or another, I have the privilege to experience this wonderful life with you.

Thank you.

Love, Mom

ACKNOWLEDGEMENTS

The biggest thanks go to my husband, Alex. For his endless support, that enabled me to make this book happen. It is incredibly rare to find someone who helps you stay grounded and at the same time allows you to fly, and accepts you just the way you are.

To my dad, the greatest grandpa, for the endless support and for the interest and willing to learn about everything I'm doing for Dan. Dad, arguing with you over different parts of this book, after you've read the draft so thoroughly, made it so much better.

To my mom, who taught me everything I know about motherhood, and whose love for me and for my children melts me every time.

To Teresa, who is always there for me with patience and love. Teresa, this book would not have been what it is today if it wasn't for you. Every time I thought I had nothing more to give, you showed me I could make it better.

To Joseph, for taking me on this amazing beautiful journey, for teaching me all these priceless lessons, and for caring so much.

To Liat Hod, for her support and for reading the manuscript over and over with so much love. Liat, your enthusiasm about the story kept me going when things got tough.

To Eyal Benvenisti, who was the first to see that my writings are going to become a book and by that made my dream real.

To Tomer Stein, for listening and for your brilliant analyzing and advice.

To Shira Stein, for helping refresh my memory about those fun days back in New York.

To Bernhard Schlink, for your thorough reading of my manuscript, and for your enlightening advice and moral support at a difficult time.

To Nira Gilad, Nina Gilson, Jennifer Smyth, Sarah Bishop, Blair Dean Cooter, Marcy Schuck, Barbara Bernstein, Diana Paulin, Renee and Brian Walker, Nancy Onofrio, and Sharon Shani for your feedback and invaluable advice. To Lindsay Walker for your great contribution.

To Sarah Bilston, for your wise counsel and feedback.

To Stephanie Kuduk-Weiner and Mark Weiner for your unwavering support. Stephanie, I will always remember how you gave me my first real lesson in writing. The fact that it was wrapped with love made it so very special.

To Sandi Shelton, for your advice, support and love, and for the great time at the writers' workshop. Edie, Marcia, and Linda: sharing my stories with you was tremendously helpful in this long process.

To the autism moms surrounding me, for your enthusiasm about my book, and your asking about it and waiting for it to happen: Loreto, Gretchen, Mary, Rena, Sandra, Marina, Heather, Chris and everyone in our group.

To Uncle Benny, who introduced me to the '10 hours a week' concept and who supported me all along the way in writing what he called "the book that no one had ever written before."

In memory of my grandpa, Chaim, who used to tell me many stories about dwarves living in the woods, and who is always with me.

Made in the USA
San Bernardino, CA
01 April 2019